Hear His Voice

Dedicated to Glen Cole
and friends at Evergreen Christian Center.

Other books by R. Douglas Wead

Tonight they'll kill a Catholic
Catholic Charismatics: Are they for real?

Hear His Voice

R. Douglas Wead

Creation House
Carol Stream, Illinois

First printing—June 1976
Second printing—November 1976

Published by Creation House, 499 Gundersen
Drive, Carol Stream, Illinois 60187
In Canada: Beacon Distributing Ltd., 104
Consumers Drive, Whitby, Ontario L1N 5T3
In Australia: Oracle Australia, Ltd., 18-26
Canterbury Road, Heathmont, Victoria 135

Biblical quotations from the *New American
Standard Bible* © 1971 are used with permission from the Lockman Foundation.

ISBN 0-88419-001-3
Library of Congress Catalog Card Number
76-16291
Printed in the United States of America

Contents

Page

Publisher's Preface   7
Preface   9

Part I   The Charismatic Renewal
1   The Mind Readers   13
2   Psychological or Spiritual Gifts?   20
3   The Acupuncture of Theology   26
4   Sources of Energy   35
5   The Gifts of the Holy Spirit   41

Part II   Operation of the Word
of Knowledge
6   The Word of Knowledge   57
7   How It Works   75
8   The Human Element   87
9   Before You Begin   100

Part III   Ministry of the Word
of Knowledge
10   The Voice of the Spirit and Healing   111
11   The Voice of the Spirit and Comfort   128
12   The Voice of the Spirit and Prophecy   143
13   The Spirit and Guidance   159
Bibliography   171

To Be Read

Does God speak to individuals today through that "still small voice" as well as through the Bible? Does He reveal His will for healing and restoration through direct communication? Or did the remarkable "word of knowledge" which God gave Old Testament prophets suddenly cease?

In accepting this book for publication, we recognize that the "word of knowledge," mentioned in I Corinthians 12:8 ("For to one is given by the Spirit the word of wisdom; to another the word of knowledge by the same Spirit"), is attracting increasing attention in the Church. But to many, its operation is mere speculation, based on hearsay.

In these pages, you will find a first-person account of the use of the "word of knowledge" today. This volume should increase understanding of spiritual gifts and encourage their development in the body of Christ.

The Publishers

Preface

When Philip announced that he had found the Christ, Nathanael responded with an insult: "Can anything good come out of Nazareth?"

Though far away, Jesus knew what Nathanael had said. How was this possible? Through what power or energy source was Jesus able to know what had happened?

Today, such a power might be referred to as a paranormal ability. Students are busy researching parapsychology, one of the newest branches of science.

But the theologians are not satisfied. As the recent charismatic renewal sweeps Protestant and Catholic Christianity, many persons are receiving these "paranormal" abilities. Most theologians will not accept that the activity is satanic; many are not satisfied that it is only a psychological phenomenon. Some are concluding that these are true gifts of God, gifts which have been used by God's people for thousands of years.

Since 1968, I have kept a careful diary of my ministry in churches and prayer groups. When I received an impression I wrote it down just as God had instructed the prophet Jeremiah.

The following account is my examination of this phenomenon. I have been careful to use actual names and places so that the stories can be verified. I have come to my conclusions slowly. I hope that this report will assist other theologians in determining the validity and practical uses of this gift of the Spirit.

Part I

The
Charismatic
Renewal

1

The Mind Readers

Susan Pfuhl was expecting her first child. For three months she had lived with the fear that she would lose the baby. Her aunt and several cousins had lost their babies and she expected the same for herself. No one knew of her anxiety, not even her husband. Yet the terror of what might happen left her weak and helpless.

Rev. Charles Jones, pastor of the Bethel Temple in Fort Worth, Texas, invited me to his church to conduct a seminar on the modern charismatic movement. During a time of prayer preceding the services, I began to receive a mental impression. I prayed for someone named Susan, whom I imagined would be in our meeting that night. Curious, I jotted down a little note, "Today I prayed for Susan; 4:30 P.M."

Hours later I'd forgotten all about Susan. While seated on the platform during the congregational singing, my eye caught a familiar face in the audience. As I tried to remember of whom she reminded me, the impressions began coming again: *This woman is expecting a baby. She is afraid that the child will be born dead. She has a family history of this. Tell her to relax. Tell her that I am with her. All will go well.* I quickly jotted down the message.

That evening following my sermon, I experienced a mysterious time of waiting. I asked those in trouble to come to the altar. People walked to the front of the sanctuary. A teenager dumped his cigarets and lighter on the altar and said he wanted God to help him give up a tobacco habit.

Finally, I could delay my curiosity no longer.

"There's someone here tonight who has great fear. God will deliver you. Identify yourself," I said.

I thought I noticed a flinch from the girl I had spotted earlier, but she did not respond. Within fifteen minutes, there were a dozen people around the altar, all exclaiming excitedly that they were the one who had fear and that they believed that God would deliver them.

The pastor began to lead the congregation in a song to cover the dilemma I had created for myself. I left twenty people praying at the altar and slipped out into the congregation to find Susan.

"Can I pray with you?" I asked. "Do you have a need?"

She seemed a bit perturbed, but when I pressed for an answer, her husband came up with something.

"Well, we could pray about my job. I may be making a change."

"I can't understand it," I said, looking back at the girl. "What's your name?"

"Sue Pfuhl," she said.

"I've been praying for someone named Susan all afternoon." I spoke with all the authority I could muster. "I have your name written down on a piece of paper in my Bible."

She broke into sobs.

"I'm the one, I'm the one, I have this fear about giving birth to our baby. My aunt lost a baby and several of my cousins lost babies."

Her husband's mouth dropped open in astonishment.

Within minutes the three of us were on the platform where Susan read aloud my notes. She was clearly identified as "the woman on the fifth row, green dress."

"God even knows my name," Susan said laughing while tears ran down her cheeks.

They were tears of joy. The past three months of fear that she had not even shared with her husband were behind her now. Susan Pfuhl had experienced an instant liberation.

Some people would dismiss this story as a freak example of extrasensory perception at work. But to a growing Christian movement involving millions of people throughout the world it is a gift of the Holy Spirit.

Theologians differ on exactly which gift it is, but it is popularly referred to as the "word of knowledge." Indeed, many Christians would be horrified to hear someone refer to it as extrasensory perception. To this Christian movement the "word of knowledge" is one of nine gifts of the Holy Spirit listed in the book of First Corinthians. Examples of these gifts or *charismas* occur throughout the entire Bible. The modern practice of and interest in them sometimes is referred to as the charismatic renewal.

The story of Susan Pfuhl did not end in that service in Fort Worth, Texas. Several weeks later my wife and I visited in the Pfuhl home. Susan had prepared a fine meal for us. She told how she was now able to sleep restfully, to eat, and to enjoy life. Her deliverance from the fear of losing her baby was complete.

One month before the baby was due to arrive, Susan was riding in the car with her husband when suddenly a Shetland pony ran in front of the car. They smashed into it, spun around uncontrollably. Terrorized, Susan reached out to her husband.

Though they had not seen me since my visit to Fort Worth many months before, in that instant they remembered the special prayer we had had together.

Pfuhl remembered the words, "I am with you; all will go well."

They had accepted those words as a message to them from God. As the car careened, he felt calmly reassured.

"The Lord is with us, Susan; all will go well," he said.

Susan relaxed. The car was demolished but Susan was not injured. One month later, their healthy baby, Katrina Sue, was born.

Originally Susan shared her need with no one. I believe that God, who knows about everyone, everywhere, not only knew of the burden, but acted to destroy it. Because He supernaturally revealed to me Susan's name, I was able to pray for her, although we had never met before. At first, God revealed only her name to me. Her actual need, a minute portion of life in the universe which is ever before the eyes of God, was still kept from me. My involvement at that point was simply to pray for Susan. Gradually, God revealed to me who she was and what her specific need was. Through this manifestation of the Holy Spirit, I was able to pray effectively for someone whom I had never met, and then to minister to her. My involvement in the event was passive. I received the supernatural revelation of the existence of Susan Pfuhl and her need so the Holy Spirit could completely deliver her.

I am convinced that God may reveal the existence, condition, or whereabouts of a person, object, or place of an event. This shared understanding of the divine mind, will or plan, edifies the body of Christ.

Ezekiel wrote of the fall of Satan as the "word of the Lord came unto me. . ." (Ezekiel 28:11). No man was witness to this event. Only God could reveal the details, and that information was the portion of His omniscience which He chose to give us.

Of course, many people cannot accept this explanation. "Isn't this ability a completely human phenomenon?" they ask. Others believe it is satanic or that God does not perform miracles and answer prayers today.

It took me many months and hundreds of personal experiences to arrive at my own firm conviction that such a "paranormal" ability is indeed one of the gifts of the Holy Spirit which the Bible refers to. I believe it is one of the gifts which appeared in the lives of the prophets as well as in the lives of Jesus and His disciples.

I agree with those who see the dangers. The prophets warn that the source of such power can be evil as well as good. Yet I am convinced that such gifts can and do occur in the lives of Christians today.

2

Psychological
or
Spiritual Gifts?

During my research and interviews with theologians, I have encountered four popular opinions about these gifts. None of them is completely satisfactory.

First, there are those people who choose to believe that such abilities do not exist at all. Despite overwhelming documentation of psychic phenomena by members of the scientific community, they believe it is all trickery and fraud. Often one example of a charlatan is used to discredit all other reports.

But this disbelief is beginning to fade as scientific interest in such phenomena increases. By 1970, the field of parapsychology was recognized by the American Association for the Advancement of Science. Scientists are becoming more disciplined in setting conditions for their experiments; thus their findings are more credible.

The revival of the occult also has been a factor in this change of popular opinion. Thousands are becoming involved in paranormal gifts, real or imagined, through the study of witchcraft.

Secondly, there are those who ascribe to the "Devil Theory." During the Watergate crisis, former White House Chief of Staff General Alexander Haig suggested that one explanation for an eighteen-and-a-half minute gap in one of the Nixon tape recordings was a "sinister force," an unknown source of energy at work. The press labeled it the "Devil Theory."

Some people dismiss as satanic anything they can not understand. In fundamentalist religious circles this view is quite common. Many believe that all modern miracles originate with Satan, regardless of the fact that such gifts appear in abundance throughout the Bible. Some, for example, suggest that anyone who claims to have the New Testament gift of speaking in tongues (the ability to pray to God spontaneously in a language one has never learned) is the result of demon possession. These same people do not believe that demons can be exorcised since that would be a miracle too. This makes speaking in tongues an incurable situation, in effect another unpardonable sin. Of course, Jesus himself was accused of performing miracles through the power of Satan.

Also there are those who believe that the emphasis on miracles is satanically inspired. Many fundamentalist pastors, for example, believe that God can perform miracles today, but that emphasizing them is dangerous because it will create a simultaneous interest by some in occult or satanic power. As public interest in psychic phenomena increased, many pastors refused to give a Biblical explanation. Experts in the occult helped fill the vacuum by offering their own theories.

A third explanation comes from those who interpret such activity as entirely spiritual. They accept that some phenomena can be satanic and they also believe in the power of God. However, these people have a tendency to reject psychological phenomena. There are no coincidences in their world. Each event is spiritualized. They attribute every phenomenon to good or evil supernatural forces.

These people usually have had a personal religious experience. Now that they have embraced the spiritual world, they tend to forget the physical world. A scientific explanation threatens them.

As a result, the scientist and the theologian continue to study the same phenomena without the cooperation of one another. They even have a different set of terms. The scientist refers to a form of psychokinesis while the theologian refers to the gifts of healing. Scientists talk about "aura"; theologians talk about "anointing."

Many people believe that studying a miracle from a physical standpoint is somehow an attack against God. Of course, this is not true. When scientists discovered the ingenious reason why Jewish infants were circumcised on the eighth day instead of the seventh or ninth, even Moses' laws seemed more miraculous. Many of the medicinal and agricultural principles behind Moses' laws have been discovered within my own lifetime. It is something of a miracle that centuries ago, God gave the Israelites such laws even though they were unable to fully appreciate the reasons for the laws.

Finally, a fourth explanation for the

gifts comes from those who believe that such activity is purely psychological.

When the gift of the word of knowledge first began to operate in my life, I immediately considered it to be a human phenomenon and not a gift of the Holy Spirit at all. Incidentally, I discovered that the gift would simply disappear during these periods of questioning. Its operation seemed to depend on my faith that it was a gift of God.

Many people have faith in a personal God and still believe that "spiritual" gifts are entirely human and psychological. They would like to keep the study of psychic phenomena separated from theology. It is almost impossible.

The Bible gives its own explanation for such gifts. There is no field of science to which the Old and New Testaments offer as much data and information as they do to the now popular field of parapsychology.

One important factor in considering the theology of gifts is the dramatic Biblical warning that such phenomena can be dangerous. While the Bible includes many beautiful stories of miracles, the Old and New Testaments both warn that such powers can be cruel. The Scriptures refer to good and evil supernatural abilities. The Bible places a strong emphasis on the motivation behind the use of such powers. Many Bible prophets who had great gifts and powers give constant warnings about the use of them.

It would be a tragedy if the scientist disregarded the warnings that come to him via the very phenomena he studies.

There may be ethical and moral considerations involved in parapsychology which no one yet fully appreciates. It may be dangerous for science to examine such secrets without also considering an ancient and wise Book written over a period of centuries by dozens of writers, many of whom were gifted with paranormal abilities.

What does the Bible say about these abilities? What is the value of a gift of the Holy Spirit such as the word of knowledge? How does the word of knowledge operate?

It would be impossible to understand this gift from a theological standpoint without first considering the whole charismatic renewal. One who understands this renewal can skip immediately to chapter six where he will begin an incredible account of this gift in operation. For those who have only begun to research, let us review one of the most fascinating religious movements in the modern day world.

3

The Acupuncture of Theology

In August 1972 I joined a group of Catholics and Protestants who were invited to Europe and Africa. We were asked to speak at colleges and in private audiences with church leaders. They wanted to know about the charismatic renewal. What was it all about and what role should it play in the church, and in the rest of the world? I did not know how to begin contributing to such a discussion.

During the exhaustive transatlantic flight to Brussels, I picked up a copy of *Newsweek.* That week presidential candidate George McGovern had dropped

Senator Thomas Eagleton from the Democratic ticket and had chosen Sargent Shriver as his new running mate. Yet the *Newsweek* cover story ignored the American political drama and focused on Chinese acupuncture.

Like others, I was intrigued by acupuncture. Only months before it was considered a superstitious oriental novelty leftover from centuries of ignorance. When members of the French medical community had studied it briefly in the 1950s, they had announced that it "worked." The rest of the Western medical profession disagreed without bothering to consider the studies. Some of the French doctors were so intimidated by their colleagues that they doubted their own facts. It was after former President Nixon's historic visit to Communist China that the world finally began to accept the idea that acupuncture works, and medical scientists in the West began to study it.

Only days after I read the *Newsweek* article I spoke to bishops, theologians and students from across Europe and Africa.

"The charismatic movement is the acupuncture of theology," I said. "It may seem bizarre or incredible but it works."

Like acupuncture, the *charismas* or gifts of the Holy Spirit have been around for a long time. At least seven of the nine gifts mentioned in I Corinthians 12 appear throughout the Old Testament, which means they have been operating for thousands of years. In the Old Testament God healed, performed miracles, and revealed His secrets through the prophets.

When young Saul began a search for several of his father's donkeys which had bolted, one of his friends suggested that they seek a prophet. "Behold now, there is a man of God in this city, and the man is held in honor; all that he says surely comes true. Now let us go there, perhaps he can tell us about our journey on which we have set out" (I Samuel 9:6). This verse suggests that the powers of God were as accessible to the common man as they were to kings.

These miraculous gifts were not given as a temporary victory for an individual, but they served as dynamic proof that God is alive and that He loves.

When Jesus appeared, He challenged people to believe that the impossible could happen. "Truly, truly, I say to you, if you shall ask the Father for anything, He will give it to you in My name. Until now you have asked for nothing in My name; ask and you will receive, that your joy may be full " (John 16:23-24).

Jesus predicted even greater power was coming: "Truly, truly, I say to you, he who believes in Me, the works that I do shall he do also; and greater works than these shall he do; because I go to the Father" (John 14:12).

After His resurrection, Jesus appeared to the disciples and told them to remain in Jerusalem to await the promise of the Holy Spirit. When the Holy Spirit arrived, the disciples were given the power to do great miracles. Later, these gifts of the Holy Spirit were given to laymen as well as to the pastors and missionaries of the early church. But sometimes there were problems; Paul cautioned the Corinthians about the misuse of the gifts.

After the second century A.D., these gifts nearly disappeared from mainstream Christianity. But not quite. There were still miracles, but these occurred as isolated incidents.

At times spiritual renewal punctuated the centuries. Sometimes renewal began because an individual was inspired by reading about the miraculous New Testament church. He would open his own life to the power of the Holy Spirit and God would forgive, heal, and speak to a whole community through him.

These revivals almost always developed problems. There were jealousies. Prophets almost always have been unpopular with their contemporaries, and many of them have been jailed or murdered.

Of course, there was the problem of the charismatic community itself. Sometimes they were so impressed by their own use of power that they refused to listen to the voice of moderation and restraint from wise church leaders. Left to themselves, they became prey to incredible extremism. The church, having learned bitter lessons from history, viewed the miraculous with skepticism. People who needed miracles were considered immature, even superstitious.

Against this backdrop of church experience, the charismatic movement of the twentieth century began.

In 1901, hundreds of communities across the United States began to experience the miraculous gifts of the Holy Spirit. The most common gift was speaking in tongues, a gift which first appeared in the upper room on the day of Pentecost when the Holy Spirit came to the disciples. Modern day charismatics were labeled Pentecostals.

The Pentecostal movement was an outrage to the established church, even to the secular world. In 1927 the president of Colgate University concluded that Pentecostalism as a religious phenomenon would occur only among people from a lower socio-economic environment. In the 1950s, many people viewed Oral Roberts's television campaign with contempt. To them it was like professional wrestling. "It is rigged, but as long as there are people who want to believe it, let them believe."

To science, the miracles were dismissed as psychological cures. Many diseases from asthma to colitis can be psychosomatic, so it was not inconceivable that psychological healings could be achieved. When science was confronted with an event it could not explain, it would simply argue that the healings were all fraudulent.

In retrospect, it seems odd that science was so hostile. What difference should it make to a medical doctor whether the cures are psychological or supernatural? If there are cures, why should not a doctor recommend prayer for a patient who has no other hope? If there are cures, should not science examine how they are achieved?

To the Pentecostals it did not matter what the theologians or scientists said. To them, the evidence was overwhelming; God was alive and He was still answering prayer. The renewal continued to spread.

The phenomenal growth of Pentecostalism has no counterpart in modern

Christianity. By 1960, the president of the New York Theological Union described it as a third force in Christendom, rivaling the Protestants and Catholics. By now, the Pentecostal movement had become international and interracial. It rivaled Buddhists in Korea and Moslems in Indonesia. In Brazil it was growing five times faster than the population and in Italy it outnumbered all other Protestants combined. In Sweden, the Pentecostals had their own political party and published the largest newspaper in the country.

But in the United States, the Pentecostal movement had serious problems.

It had begun in rural frontier America and had become a captive of its own unique culture. Handclapping, shouting and hyperemotionalism characterized its worship services. Pentecostals, no matter how popular they were in rural America, were obnoxious to mainstream Christianity where they were referred to as "holy rollers." That was to change.

The changes that took place in Pentecostalism can, in large measure, be attributed to the population trends of the 1900s. In 1920, thirty percent of the American population lived and worked on farms. By 1970, that figure was reduced to five percent for millions of Americans had moved to the cities. With them had come the Pentecostals.

Not only did the city influence the Pentecostal movement, but the Pentecostal movement was beginning to move in on the city. When disaster came to an individual in the form of bankruptcy, divorce, or illness, a Pentecostal was there to recommend a miracle. Pentecostalism spread like a forest fire through the suburbs. The suburban neo-Pentecostals believed that the power of God had indeed been given to these "holy rollers" they had once despised, but they did not want to embrace the peculiar rural Pentecostal culture. They remained Baptists, Lutherans, Episcopalians, Presbyterians, and Catholics. Their numbers grew by the thousands.

By 1970 nearly every national periodical was reporting the phenomenon. One by one traditional Protestant church denominations reluctantly endorsed what they called the "charismatic renewal." In 1974, 40,000 delegates attended the annual Catholic Pentecostal conference at Notre Dame University.

The common denominator of the renewal was a "Christ experience" or the born-again experience. This experience enabled a person to know by faith that Christ had really died for his sins and that

He was alive today. Then, of course, came the gifts of the Holy Spirit.

4

Sources of Energy

If we are going to examine the word of knowledge we must first consider all the other gifts. This is especially important because the gifts of the Holy Spirit often work in conjunction with one another. Even the best definitions of these gifts tend to overlap.

In I Corinthians 12 nine gifts of the Holy Spirit are listed:

For to one is given the word of wisdom through the Spirit, and to another the word of knowledge according to the same Spirit; to another faith by the same Spirit, and to another gifts of healing by the one Spirit, and to another the effecting of miracles, and to another prophecy, and to another the distinguishing of spirits, to another various kinds of tongues, and to another the interpretation of tongues. But one and the same Spirit works all these things, distributing to each one individually just as He wills (verses 8-11).

Before giving some of the popular definitions of these charismas, I should explain that charismatics believe that all these gifts are supernatural. As supernatural gifts, they cannot be earned or developed, although human mechanics are involved.

The whole molecular structure of the universe is positive, negative, and neutral. In the spiritual world there is a positive and negative too. There is God which in this illustration I represent as positive, and there is evil which I represent as negative. There is also the physical world and the human spirit, which are neutral and feel the tension between the two forces.

With this illustration in mind, consider the gifts of the Holy Spirit. There is the word of wisdom, a supernatural gift of

God. There is also a counterfeit to this gift which has as its source an evil or satanic energy. Finally, there is a human counterpart to the gift of the word of wisdom—human wisdom. This is critically important. There cannot be supernatural if there is not a natural. Below are listed the nine gifts and a human counterpart for each.

Positive: God's gifts of the Holy Spirit	Neutral: Some human counterparts	Negative: There is also a satanic counterpart to each gift
word of wisdom	human wisdom, psychology	The satanic counterparts are forgeries of the gifts of the Spirit. Thus someone may magically effect a cure (healing) or may spontaneously speak another language (tongues) through satanic energy. Each of the gifts of the Spirit may be counterfeited.
word of knowledge	human knowledge	
faith	positive thinking	
gifts of healing	medicine	
working of miracles	technology	
prophecy	electronic communications, prediction of wars, hurricanes, earthquakes	
discerning of spirits	psychoanalysis	
speaking in tongues	learning foreign languages	
interpretation of tongues	interpretation of languages	

For example, notice the working of miracles, a gift of the Holy Spirit, and its human or natural counterpart, which I have listed as technology. Man cannot fly, yet through the miracle of technology, he does. The Boeing 747 is not a gift of the Holy Spirit nor is it evil, but it is a miracle of human technology and scientific engineering.

Another example is the supernatural gift of prophecy. It also has a human counterpart. Men have been able to predict wars, presidential elections, hurricanes, even earthquakes. These "prophecies" are declared on television and in the press. The methods have been natural, not supernatural.

Let me give one more example. There is the gift of discerning of spirits. A good analyst or psychiatrist can eventually isolate and identify the various personalities in an individual who believes he is demon-possessed. Some theologians would refer to these personalities as demons. The scientist would interpret the situation as acute schizophrenia. The scientist's ability to determine the personalities takes place after many hours of observation and many interviews. It is not a gift of the Holy Spirit nor is the psychiatrist's work satanic. Through the gift of discerning of spirits the same thing can be achieved in seconds. Natural becomes supernatural.

However, there is a satanic or evil counterpart to each of the gifts. Someone may speak in tongues through the inspiration of evil power rather than the Holy Spirit's power. Such phenomena have occurred.

The difficulty comes in drawing the line between the different areas. There are moments when the word of knowledge may operate in a dramatic way. Someone who has no paranormal abilities at all may through the Holy Spirit know information about people which helps him pray for them. The detail of the information may reach well beyond any possibility of coincidence. There are other occasions when it is difficult to know if a gift of the Holy Spirit has operated. A pastor may preach a sermon which one individual will say was definitely for him. It might be difficult to determine whether this was the result of the pastor's excellent preparation and keen insight into the problems of his people, or whether there was actually a gift in operation.

There are situations where it is equally difficult to distinguish between human phenomena and a miracle of the occult.

Not only are there different sources for miracles, but the Bible also teaches there are different operations of the gifts (I Corinthians 12:6).

The gifts of the Holy Spirit operate or are used in different ways. Without getting into the human mechanics, I should point out the relationship between the love chapter (I Corinthians 13) and the gifts of the Holy Spirit. Chapter 13 is sandwiched between two other chapters dealing with charismas. The message of the chapter is that love is more important than the operation of gifts. Miracles must be motivated by compassion or they lose their significance. When the gifts of the Holy Spirit operate in love, they are overwhelming. When they operate without it, they appear flashy and artificial.

5

The Gifts of
the Holy Spirit

(1) The most important gift of the Holy Spirit is the *word of wisdom*. Many Christians believe this gift is supernatural. The word of wisdom is not human wit, such as when Jesus answered the Pharisees' question about taxes by saying that Caesar's picture is on the coin so "give to Caesar what belongs to Caesar."

An example of supernatural wisdom is Jesus' statement to Nicodemus, "You must be born again."

The entire second chapter of I Corinthians distinguishes between man's wisdom and the wisdom of God. In this sense, the word of wisdom is the ability to see and explain it as God would, to understand priorities. This does not belittle the practical wisdom of man as expressed by Solomon in Proverbs. Man's wisdom must be learned and pursued, but the gift of the word of wisdom is a revelation of God's wisdom and sometimes defies human understanding.

Those who exercise the gifts of the Spirit do not claim that the gift of the word of wisdom is a recent invention of God's. They contend that the gift has operated unrecognized in Christian communities for years.

Few charismatic theologians are dogmatic in their definition of what the gift actually is. However, what has emerged as the popular concept of the word of wisdom does have certain characteristics. In a prayer community, it comes constructively as a gentle explanation or suggestion rather than as a criticism. Almost always, it refers to a Scripture.

(2) The *"word" of knowledge* is translated from the Greek term *logos*, meaning word, matter or concern. It is a revelation of knowledge, not an utterance or writing. It is a thought which may be expressed either audibly or visually; it

represents an infinitesimal portion of the whole knowledge of God. Sometimes God uses it to reveal His will for a person or situation.

Some confuse the gift of the word of knowledge with natural ability. If this gift and natural talent are synonymous, the word of knowledge would no longer be a supernatural occurrence and would not have been referred to in I Corinthians as a manifestation of the Spirit.

Others consider the word of knowledge to be the result of profound study of the Bible and theology. It would then be limited to mature, knowledgeable men of God. In that case, however, young Samuel, to whom God gave a message for Eli, the priest, could not have been instrumental in delivering God's word. It is not the product of long experience in the ways and doings of the Lord; even the young and inexperienced may be used.

Most theologians in the charismatic movement may feel that my definition is incomplete; that the word of knowledge is a spiritual gift given to assist the teaching ministry. To them, this gift enables a minister to remember or to know his material better; he can miraculously preach the perfect sermon for a particular situation. Charismatic theologians believe that the gift of a legitimate heavenly extrasensory perception should be categorized differently.

Some Catholic theologians refer to the ability to know details about someone else through supernatural means as "prophetic utterance," a function of the gift of prophecy. Many Protestant theologians refer to it as a function of the gift of miracles. In spite of these opinions, most laymen in the charismatic movement still refer to it as the word of knowledge.

I do not define it exactly or dogmatically. Though this supernatural ability appears throughout the Bible, no occasion in Scripture identifies it as one particular gift of the Holy Spirit. Arguments that it is really a prophetic gift are no more convincing to me than the popular definition that it is the word of knowledge. I have decided to yield to this "layman concept" in order to communicate.

(3) The *gift of faith*: God has given to every man a measure of faith, but this gift is an exceptional ability enabling one to believe and accept a miracle.

The gift of faith can be distinguished from the working of miracles or from the gifts of healing. When the woman with the issue of blood touched the hem of Jesus' garment, Jesus was not initiating a gift of healing or working of miracles. Through the word of knowledge He knew something had happened. He stopped and said, "Who touched My garments?" (Mark 5:30). The woman was found and she explained how she had been healed simply by touching Jesus' robe.

Our Lord's comment to this woman was, "Your faith has made you well" (5:34). The woman's faith was a gift of the Holy Spirit. The miraculous and healing ministry of Jesus often stirred the gift of faith into action. On many occasions, Jesus did not even pray for a situation, but simply commented as He did to the woman with the issue of blood, "Your faith has made you well."

The Holy Spirit's gift of faith then can be distinguished from the God-given faith which every man can use to believe in His plan for them.

(4) *Gifts of healing:* Perhaps no gifts of the Holy Spirit are as popular as the gifts of healing. It is interesting to consider how sympathetic most Christian laymen have been to this concept.

While some conservative fundamentalist pastors teach that the day of miracles ended with the death of the last apostle, many of their parishioners could point to exceptions. While they may not feel any kinship to the wild Pentecostal movement around them, they often pray for someone they love when there is a sickness. Sometimes there appear to be results.

The theologians were usually cynical about any reported answers to prayer but, especially in the Episcopalian and Lutheran churches, there was scholarly curiosity. Movements began which studied and experimented in divine healing. This made it much more difficult to deny the other gifts of the Holy Spirit when they began to occur in mainstream Christianity.

(5) The *working of miracles*: The actual Greek word is *dunamis*, which means power. The displays of power occur at special times when laws of nature are temporarily suspended and a miracle takes place. One example is Jesus' walking on the water.

Faith is passive, the ability to receive; the working of miracles is active. An individual takes the initiative and the miraculous happens.

These are not frequent occurrences, of course, or they would not be considered miracles. Like gold, a working of great power is valuable because it is rare. In this sense, God seems to discipline Himself in reserving the use of such gifts for special occasions.

(6) The *gift of prophecy*: The gift of

prophecy is a supernatural gift which allows a person to communicate the truths of God with great effect. Sometimes it is referred to as "anointing." It is not bound by time, and sometimes a prophet will speak of events which have not yet happened.

One can be anointed in simple conversation or even while singing, as well as while addressing an audience. In describing how it feels to be "anointed," some ministers refer to warmth, others refer to enthusiasm.

But there are definite problems involving prophecy and guidance which I will detail in later chapters. The Bible constantly warns against false prophets, and it gives at least four guidelines in determining whether a prophecy is of God or not.

First, if the prophecy speaks of future events which do not take place, the Bible says, "the Lord has not spoken. The prophet has spoken it presumptuously; you shall not be afraid of him" (Deuteronomy 18:22). Unfortunately, one has to wait to see if a prophet is speaking for God.

Second, Jesus said that we could recognize good and false prophets by the examination of the effects of their ministry (Matthew 7:15-17).

Third, the Holy Spirit has given to the church the gift of discerning of spirits which can immediately unmask a fraud (I Corinthians 12:10). Finally, the apostle John declares that we can test the spirits to see if they are from God or not. The explanation of this test is found in I John 4:1-3.

(7) The *discerning of spirits*: The discerning or distinguishing of spirits is a supernatural look into the spiritual world. The gift enables one to determine whether a source of inspiration in an individual is God, if it is evil, or if it is only the human spirit.

For some time I assumed that this gift operated quite obviously. Everyone in a prayer group, for example, would sense when something was right or wrong. But this gift also may operate in a highly sophisticated manner.

I remember an occasion when a prominent visitor attended one of our seminars. During a question and answer session, he posed some provocative questions.

One member of the local congregation cornered me after the seminar.

"Did you notice anything strange about the gentleman who asked all the questions?" he asked.

Oh no, I thought, *here is one of those*

fanatical charismatics who sees demons everywhere he looks. I had thought that the gentleman's questions were stimulating and made good discussion. But the man insisted something was wrong.

The next day we all heard a strange story. Our visitor of the previous evening had gone to a baptismal ceremony that day. As godfather to the infant, he had to participate by repeating a simple confession of Christ. Suddenly he was mute. In a quiet and unobtrusive way, the priest touched the man's arm. Quietly he said, "In the name of Jesus, come out of him!"

He had acted in experimentation, thinking that his prayer would be harmless and might have some effect. The man he prayed for suddenly threw a fit; he screamed. The ceremony was totally disrupted and everyone who had witnessed the incident was badly shaken.

The next night the visitor returned to our seminar. His face was aglow as he testified that he evidently had been delivered of an evil spirit. The local associate pastor and I were skeptical. We contacted the priest.

"Yes, it happened," he said, "but I don't understand it and I don't know if I want to. I will admit it to you but please don't talk about it. We are trying to hush the thing up."

The experience was especially intriguing to me. The man involved was a prominent businessman. Two of his employees, who were active in our seminar, came to me later.

"We had no idea that there was anything wrong with him," they said. "And we have worked with him for several years."

I had noticed nothing strange about him, either. Yet, a member of the local congregation had discerned something immediately and had tried to tell me about it.

The same thing occurred in the life of the Apostle Philip. Among his many converts at Samaria was Simon. The Bible says that Simon believed and was baptized. Then Peter and John arrived. Peter immediately discerned something about Simon that even Philip had not. He rebuked Simon saying, "I see that you are in the gall of bitterness and in the bondage of iniquity" (Acts 8:23).

(8) *Various kinds of tongues:* None of the gifts of the Holy Spirit is as controversial as the gift of speaking in tongues. The Bible teaches that there are different kinds of tongues. This gift allows a person to speak spontaneously in a language he has never previously learned.

The human mechanics of speaking in tongues are quite simple and may even seem foolish. The miracle is that God can take something foolish as glossalalia, give it utterance and make it sing like a beautiful language. It is another case of God using a foolish thing to confound the wisdom of man.

There is a gift of tongues that is directed to unbelievers. On the day of Pentecost, the disciples began to speak in many languages. When the international visitors to the Jewish Pentecost festival heard their own language, they were amazed.

The great American explorer, Marquette, records having spoken to Indian tribes in their own languages through a miracle of the Holy Spirit.

In his book, *For This Cross I'll Kill You*, Bruce Olson refers to the time when the Motilone Indians preached Christ to the Yuko tribe which lived only ten miles away. The Motilones and Yukos had been rivals and had not communicated with each other for generations. Their language differences were extremely complicated; one language was tonal, the other was not. Yet through a gift of the Holy Spirit, the Motilones were able to speak to their neighboring tribe about Christianity.

A fascinating event occurred while I

was conducting a seminar at Glad Tidings Church in San Francisco. During a time of worship, the entire congregation began singing together in prayer languages. Evidently my voice was carrying over the public address system.

After the service I was approached by a young lady. "Where did you learn Hebrew?" she asked.

"I don't know any Hebrew."

"Well, you were singing in it tonight."

I thought that she was a fanatical Pentecostal who had taken a couple of night courses in Hebrew and thought she had heard a familiar syllable.

I was wrong. She was Pat Laudenslager who, as a Jew, was attending a Christian church for the first time in her life. Naturally she was curious about what had happened. This gave Pastor Floyd Thomas and a friend who had brought Pat to the church a chance to talk about Christianity.

Some charismatics would include a prayer language in the gift of tongues. Others say that the prayer language is something separate. The Apostle Paul wrote, "One who speaks in a tongue does not speak to men, but to God; for no one understands, but in his spirit he speaks mysteries" (I Corinthians 14:2). Later he says, "What is the outcome then? I shall pray with the spirit and I shall pray with the mind also; I shall sing with the spirit and I shall sing with the mind also" (I Corinthians 14:15).

Finally, there is a message in tongues which is given publicly. The Apostle Paul warns that to give a public demonstration of a language requires an interpretation. If there is no one there to interpret, the message in tongues should not be given (I Corinthians 14:27, 28).

Speaking in tongues appears to be quite bizarre and mysterious to many who first encounter it, usually because of the extreme emotion which accompanies this event in many classical Pentecostal congregations. However, when speaking in tongues occurs in a quiet and gentle way, most people can understand how simple and natural such an expression really is.

(9) The *interpretation of tongues* is an ability to relate what an individual has spoken in his language. When a message in tongues and an interpretation has been given, it will produce a result similar to that of prophecy (I Corinthians 14:5).

It is important to note that this is not a gift of translation. The message in tongues will not be translated word for word, but rather will be interpreted. Therefore, the interpreter tends to use his own vocabulary in expressing what has been said.

It is amusing to see someone with the gift of interpretation develop a cliche to preface his actual interpretation. Someone may begin an interpretation with the words, "My little children," or some other King James English phrase. This is unnecessary, of course, but it happens.

I have given only a brief introduction to the gifts of the Holy Spirit. Much of what I have said is still quite debatable among theologians. Yet, right or wrong, these definitions represent popular opinion as I have found it in the charismatic movement today.

Part II

Operation of the Word of Knowledge

6

The Word of Knowledge

"The fellowship of the Holy Spirit be with you all."

So Paul ended his second letter to the church at Corinth. This *koinonia* is the joint participation of the Christian with the Holy Spirit around their common interest in Jesus Christ.

All things in the experience of Christians should lead to this ultimate: "to be conformed to the image of His Son" (Romans 8:29), to mirror Christ. Here is the basic purpose of the gifts of the Spirit, to bring us into Christlikeness in character, mind, work and word. The gifts of revelation, discerning of spirits, word of wisdom, and word of knowledge are given so that man may participate to an infinitesimal degree in the omniscience of God.

What is the ministry of Christ to the world? The charismatic Christian believes that his ministry is directed to both the spiritual and physical needs of man. Similarly Jesus, when asked to name the greatest law of Moses, replied, " 'You shall love the Lord your God with all your heart, and with all your soul, and with all your mind.' The second is like it, 'You shall love your neighbor as yourself.' " (Matthew 19:37, 39).

The first priority in the life of a Christian is his relationship to God. In this sense the charismatic movement is highly evangelical. The emphasis is on a Christ experience or "new birth." When Roman Catholics take the "Life in the Spirit" seminar the Christ experience is emphasized. Classical Pentecostals believe that what is referred to as the Christ experience is actually salvation, the new birth or the equivalent of baptism. (Classical Pentecostals teach that water baptism by immersion should symbolize the "salvation experience," but the actual practice is to emphasize the Christ experience. Some classical Pentecostal converts are not even informed of water baptism until weeks later.) In this sense the gifts of the Holy Spirit are powerful in provoking man to make a decision about God.

"This One is indeed the Savior of the world" (John 4:42). So the Samaritans testified to their encounter with Jesus during His two-day visit. They came to Him because of the witness of a woman who had met Him outside of the village. She described their encounter at Jacob's well where the stranger had demonstrated great power by describing the personal life of the woman He never had seen before. She recognized Him to be a prophet because of the word of knowledge He had given her. He told her that He was the Christ. In the village, she testified to many of this encounter with the Savior and they believed on Him, begging Him to remain with them several days.

Today, the Holy Spirit is working in the same manner to bring people to God through a Christ-experience.

During the spring of 1974 I was part of a team conducting a seminar in Albany, Oregon. An Episcopalian shared the workshop with me. Before walking out onto the platform, the Holy Spirit showed me a young lady in the audience. She was in great spiritual trouble. In my mind I saw her face, where she was sitting, and what she was wearing. The Holy Spirit gave me instructions; He told me what to say to her and how to help her.

When the worship service began, I walked out into the sanctuary. There she was, sitting right where the Holy Spirit had indicated.

At the conclusion of the service I went to her and said, "You've been praying about something special, haven't you?"

"Yes, I've been asking God to give me the gift of the Holy Spirit."

I showed her a note I had written on paper. It described what she was wearing and where she was sitting. I had written the words, "She will say she wants the gift of the Holy Spirit."

The young lady looked at the note with a puzzled expression on her face as if she were thinking, *Can God really give me the Holy Spirit in spite of the way I'm living?*

"There's more," I said. "You're not even serving God. The man you live with is not your husband. God is going to clean you up. He is going to forgive your sins and give you joy. You did not really know what you were talking about when you asked for the gift of the Holy Spirit, but that is exactly what you are going to get. Jesus is going to baptize you in His Spirit tonight and you will never be the same."

I led her to the center of the room. Then I told the audience that they were witnessing a miracle of salvation and invited them to join me in celebrating the moment.

Pastor Earl Book and the other ministers came. We anointed her with oil and she was baptized in the Holy Spirit. Before the week was concluded, she personally led two other friends to Christ.

In the summer of 1972, I was guest speaker for a three-week church youth camp program in upstate New York. I don't specialize in youth ministry, and I felt especially handicapped working with a large group of city kids who seemed determined not to participate in anything which might directly influence them spiritually.

I was walking down the steps from my room to the chapel. The Holy Spirit had been speaking to me all day. *This is going to be a critical service. For some of the kids it will be make or break. It is important. Preach a simple evangelistic message.*

Tension began to rise. *How am I going to get these kids from the city to respond at the altar? I'm no good with youth anyway. I just don't know what to do.*

So, I asked God for a sign.

"Give me some sort of sign so I can demonstrate to them the importance of this service," I prayed.

The number twenty-two came to my thoughts, but I did not know what it meant. Perhaps twenty-two people would respond, or maybe row twenty-two in the chapel would be significant. It was just an impression, but I did not reject it completely. If it were of God, He would be more specific.

I was sitting on the platform before the service that evening, thumbing through the chorus book. Again, the impression twenty-two came to me. So I turned to page twenty-two and read "When the Roll Is Called Up Yonder." This was a southern song which I had not heard a congregation sing in many years. Yet an impression came. *They're going to sing this song in the service. When they begin, interrupt them and tell them the importance of this service.*

I wrote the message down in ink in the songbook. Cal, the camp director from Glens Falls, New York, and his brother sang a special medley which included "When The Roll Is Called Up Yonder." I stood up and interrupted them. With a brief explanation, I had Cal read the note and then the medley was concluded.

My audience listened with rapt attention that night. Some of them were trying to decide what my interruption was all about. Was it some kind of trick?

At my conclusion, dozens of youth expressed a spiritual need for the first time during that week of camp. Most prayed for a Christ-experience. It was the beginning of the end for those who were holding out on Jesus.

In the same way that the word of knowledge had reached a village of Samaritans, many teen-agers responded to Jesus following this manifestation of the Spirit.

Perhaps the most practical use of the word of knowledge for evangelism is in a one-to-one relationship. In counseling, the Holy Spirit can help a pastor eliminate hours of talking by showing him the real problem.

Such a situation occurred at the Evergreen Christian Center in Olympia, Washington. Pastor Glen Cole arranged a counseling session for two young ladies. They wanted to talk with me about an evil spirit which was tormenting one of them. I asked my wife, Gloria, to join me. We met the girls one afternoon at the church.

The story was that one of the girls had been experiencing moments of violent temper. She would throw things around the apartment and lose all reason. Her frightened roommate had talked her into seeking help. As we listened to the story politely, Gloria thought it might be a psychological problem. The motion picture version of *The Exorcist* had just been released in the area, and there was a rash of demon stories.

But the Holy Spirit had instantly revealed to me the true nature of the problem.

"Are you two in love?" I asked.

A long pause answered the question. One of the girls broke into tears.

"I was hoping the Lord would show you. I just couldn't bear to tell anyone," she said.

The two girls were having a difficult time reconciling their homosexuality to their faith in the Word of God. We got right to the point and discussed the problem at great length. After a prayer of deliverance, I gave some rather lengthy practical instructions.

In spite of our prayers and long talk, I must admit that I was not anticipating dramatic results. I was to be surprised. Within a week they had moved away from each other. One girl was attempting to return to her husband; the other seemed to be at peace with herself. The painful process of reorientation was actually taking place in their lives.

A revelation from the Holy Spirit makes the difference in a situation like that. Many problems are so complex that the idea of an omniscient and omnipotent God who can help us provides the extra courage needed to make the right decision.

On other occasions the voice of the Spirit can expose sin. David repented when Nathan by the power of the Holy Spirit described the murder of Uriah which preceded David's marriage to Bathsheba.

Naaman the Syrian was a leper who sought healing from the prophet Elisha. When he dipped in the Jordan and was completely healed, he returned to the prophet, desiring to give thanks for his healing. Elisha refused payment for the work of the Lord. But his servant Gehazi returned to Naaman asking gifts in the name of his master which he then hid away for himself. God showed Elisha Gehazi's sin and he became a leper, a grave punishment.

King Jeroboam sent his wife, disguised as a peasant, to the prophet Ahijah to learn if their sick child would live or die. Jeroboam had sinned against God in his rule over Israel, and because of his sin he feared that Ahijah would not tell him the truth. But the prophet was not deceived, for the Lord came to him warning of the approach of the king's wife and foretelling the impending doom of Jeroboam's family.

In the early Church, the Holy Spirit operated to reveal sin and to bring spiritual growth to the young body of Christians. Ananias and Sapphira foolishly attempted to appear generous to the believers when in an act of giving they lied to God. The Holy Spirit revealed to Peter their thievery and both were struck dead as demonstration to the Church of the seriousness of tempting God.

Nabyte is the Arabic name given to an old missionary woman who lived for thirty years in Jerusalem. On many occasions the Holy Spirit had spoken words of guidance to her. One time He helped her do a little detective work.

Nabyte lived with a house full of young people. Many of them were orphans, others were abandoned children, and the rest were children of missionaries. A serious problem developed when a visiting guest was robbed. Nabyte knew that the white missionary children had the best opportunity to steal from the guest, yet after having used all her skill at interrogation, she was no closer to an answer for the problem.

"That night I went to bed. I told God that I just had to know one way or another."

When Nabyte awakened the next morning she knew. "It was clear-cut," she says. "I don't know how I knew but I did. I was convinced. It was the oldest Arabic child."

Nabyte had cared for the Arabic girl since infancy. Her father had begged Nabyte to take his child; one of his children already had died of starvation. Nabyte took the Arabic girl and soon afterwards the father himself died.

When the girl entered Nabyte's room to dust the furniture, Nabyte cornered her.

"You took it!" She said with her hands on her hips and a scowl on her face.

The oldest Arabic girl was stunned. "Yes," she said, "I did!"

Others had been accused of the crime so the Arabic girl was ordered to straighten it out, which she did.

Nabyte and her powerful gift from God made quite an impression on the people in the house. In spite of the bitter politics of the Middle East, each of the children eventually embraced the Christian faith. The oldest Arabic child now lives in Jordan and is married to a wealthy pharmacist.

Nabyte is the Arabic word which means "prophetess."

On many occasions God gives direct knowledge about an individual so one will know how to pray for him or how to influence him toward devotion to God. Even the gifts of healing and the working of miracles stimulate faith and achieve a spiritual purpose much deeper than the particular physical problem they are affecting at the moment.

Besides their evangelical purpose, however, the gifts of the Holy Spirit are excellent tools for loving and ministering to other people. The last half of the commandment—"Love your neighbor as yourself"—becomes the motivation behind the use of such gifts.

Arlene Jackson, a beautiful twenty-eight-year-old Baptist who had a Christ-experience in 1970, began to hear reports of the charismatic movement. Arlene had experienced some deep emotional confusion and often was overcome with depression. She wondered if God could help her with these problems just as He had so dramatically changed her spiritual life. It seemed as though prayers were answered for other people but never for herself.

The more she read the Bible, the more she longed for an answer. Arlene also had a secret prayer which she shared with no one. For most of her life, she had been deaf in one ear. After reading a book about the charismatic movement, Arlene Jackson asked God to give her complete hearing. Such a fantastic request would have seemed presumptuous to her Baptist friends, but Arlene maintained her secret desire for a miracle.

Emotional problems and depression continued to plague Arlene. On one occasion she was hospitalized. In spite of the fact that she felt she was in spiritual harmony with God and others, the desperate emotional and psychological problems persisted. Arlene was trying to have faith. She was trying to believe that God really cared about her physical problems too.

In September 1973, Arlene attended a Kathryn Kuhlman evangelistic meeting in Jacksonville. She practiced for weeks so she would be able to sing in the choir and get a seat at the large auditorium.

"It was a beautiful day," Arlene remembers. "There was no miracle in my life, but it was wonderful to see other people helped. It felt so good. 'This is the way I ought to feel all the time,' I thought."

Months later Arlene was in the hospital. Severe depression had set in again. She became disillusioned with her prayer life. This time she was hospitalized eleven days before doctors sent her home. There seemed to be no other hope for her but God.

In May 1973, I was invited to Jacksonville, Florida where the Rev. Dale Zink had arranged an interdenominational charismatic conference. He checked me into the Holiday Inn, and I spent the rest of the afternoon in prayer. During prayer, the Holy Spirit began to show me Arlene Jackson and I began to write my impressions.

In later chapters I will explain in detail why I like to write on paper what I feel are God's messages. Too often, as an "inside" observer of the charismatic movement, I suspected that Pentecostal leaders used psychology and clever words to give the effect of "knowing personal problems." Or an evangelist would use the power of suggestion. He would say, "Twelve people will come to the altar tonight!" Of course he would be right. We would wait thirty minutes until the twelfth person would respond and the thirteenth was not about to come. It would have seemed as though he were out of God's will. As a Pentecostal preacher's son, I did not believe that these actions were purposeful or fraudulent, but I resented it anyway.

My criticisms were unconstructive. Yet when I finally became involved in the use of the gifts myself, I determined to operate them in a way that would convince some of the skeptical people in the audience. If I received an impression that twelve people would respond, I would put it on paper and let it happen without any public announcements. Then I could show them how awesome God's sovereignty really is and how important the twelve people are in God's eyes.

I described Arlene Jackson on paper as I imagined I would see her at the conference that evening. She would be wearing a green dress; she is partially deaf. I groped for more details.

What row is she on? I looked carefully at the picture in my mind. I counted the rows of pews. She was sitting on the sixth row.

Hours later, I left my written message in Pastor Zink's office and walked into the sanctuary with him.

"There is someone here who is partially deaf," I told the audience. "God will heal you if you believe. Come to the front."

An elderly lady walked down the aisle on my left.

"There is someone else," I called.

Arlene Jackson was there that night. She was sitting on the sixth row and she was wearing a green dress, just as I had seen her. She hesitated a moment, then stepped into the aisle and came to the front of the room.

"She is the one," I said, pointing to the woman in the green dress walking down the aisle.

I invited the deacons and the pastor to pray with me. We used special anointing oil to touch her forehead and then laid hands on her in the same way that deacons of the New Testament church prayed for the sick.

The organist was playing softly in the background. Suddenly Arlene felt the music swirl around her in beautiful stereophonic. She was overjoyed. "It is happening," she told the audience, "it is really happening!"

Several evenings later, I was seated on the platform during the preliminaries of the evening service. I glanced out into the audience and Arlene's anguished face caught my eye.

What is wrong, Lord? I prayed.

There is more than just deafness. There is a much deeper problem, He answered.

Despite the great miracle Arlene Jackson had experienced, she was still not completely free from her emotional confusion. After her experience, she had assumed that the depression would be gone forever. But in some lonely moments she had panicked. Her joy of a miracle had somehow been stolen from her. She had concluded that perhaps there was no hope for her after all.

Once more I called her from the audience. "God has begun a great work in you and Satan is trying to defeat it. He will not succeed. Jesus has healed you and He will deliver you from all your fears," I said.

A rich and warm presence of Christ was with us. I touched her forehead lightly with oil. Arlene suddenly collapsed and fell to the floor. I had not intended to sensationalize the moment, but I let her lie peacefully. No one moved.

The congregation had been standing, so I led them in singing. Five hundred voices filled the sanctuary. I saw Arlene singing with us in a beautiful language.

In November, I returned to Jacksonville, to conduct a special Thanksgiving service for Pastor Zink. Arlene cornered me after the service with a bright smile. "Do you remember me?"

"Of course! What's been happening to you?"

"Sit down and I'll tell you," she said excitedly. "The Holy Spirit has been at work in my life. I have more confidence."

There had still been ups and downs but Arlene was beginning to understand herself and even more importantly, she was reaching out to others.

It is hard for me to explain the joy that comes from seeing people helped. It is especially rewarding to return later and see that there is more to the gifts of the Holy Spirit than just an emotional moment. God uses these mysterious charismas in many profound ways. Perhaps the effect is subconscious, I don't know. I do know that if we open our lives to Christ's power, He will work through us to love and heal other people.

7

How It Works

I believe the key to the operation of the gifts of the Holy Spirit is simplicity.

Those who have a prayer language know for a fact that the human mechanics are very easy, almost foolish. The mystery is that God can use something as simple as speaking in tongues to heighten our spiritual experience. The Holy Spirit provides what the Scriptures call "utterance" and suddenly the words seem to sing like a beautiful language.

In my book, *Catholic Charismatics*, I document a story of a woman who speaks in Portuguese when the Holy Spirit prays through her. To her knowledge, she has never been exposed to the Portuguese language. When she prays in tongues, she merely speaks the words which pour from her subconscious. To people who speak in tongues it is so simple, yet at the same time it is profound.

So it is with all the gifts. God has chosen the foolish things to confound the mighty.

Though I had experienced a prayer language in my private devotions years before, it has only been in recent years that I began to discover that the other spiritual gifts operate just as easily.

I was working with my father as his assistant pastor in a large classical Pentecostal church. I realized that sooner or later as a pastor I would have to have the gift of interpretation. To classical Pentecostal mentality, it is inconceivable that a pastor can lead a worship service without it. So, I began to consider it, think about it, and talk about it. I came to the conclusion that interpretation is probably as simple as speaking in tongues in the first place. So I asked God to give me the gift of interpretation.

One Sunday morning, there was a message in tongues in the service and the Holy Spirit began to speak to me: *You wanted the gift of interpretation, all right, interpret.*

Wait a minute, I argued. *Now, how do I know this is God? What should I say?*

So, I made an agreement with God. If no one interpreted, I would believe that He was speaking to me and that He wanted me to interpret.

Now I don't think asking for a fleece is a good thing to do, but God gave it to me. There was a long awkward pause with admonitions from the pastor for the interpretation. And though there were many who had the gift of interpretation, no one exercised it.

That night in the service, there was another message in tongues, and I realized that I had the interpretation. I had to give it. The same arguments came. But this time with boldness and confidence, I formulated the whole paragraph before I spoke it. I thought it over several times, choosing my words because I wanted it to be beautiful. I gave my interpretation, and when I finished, the anointing of the Holy Spirit was strong in a tremendous confirmation!

Years later I began a study of the gifts of the Holy Spirit. When I came to the word of knowledge I was confused. I had always resented the popular concept of the word of knowledge. I felt that it was a poor definition.

I could not identify with the way it

seemed to operate, either. Very often, a Pentecostal evangelist would say, "Someone here has fear."

Well, chances are high that hundreds of people in a large audience have a phobia about something. It did not impress me. At other times, the evangelist would say, "Someone over on this side of the sanctuary has had pains in his chest."

But everyone has had pains in his chest at some time. So someone would always respond, and this would be referred to as a miracle of the word of knowledge.

My cynical attitude was unconstructive and perhaps immature from a Christian standpoint. If I did not like the way a certain gift was operating, I should have provided a better example. Instead, I only criticized everyone else.

When one begins to write, however, something happens. He becomes very objective. He begins to challenge some of his own views and to reconsider some of the theories he so easily dismissed before.

I began to reconsider the popular classical Pentecostal concept of the word of knowledge. It was strange. Few of the contemporary charismatic theologians agreed with the "heavenly ESP" theory—yet it persisted among involved laymen and ministers.

If this is what is meant by the gift of the

Holy Spirit, it would be more common, I thought. *It would not be reserved for great prophets or important men of God. The gifts of the Spirit are for the whole church.*

Yet at the same time, I knew that this phenomenon occurred frequently in Scripture. The fact that it was a rare occurrence today could be our fault, not the Holy Spirit's.

During this time of personal debate, I was conducting a seminar in Jacksonville, Florida, with Pastor Paul Goodman. One Sunday night, while I was sitting on the platform, an interesting thought struck me. If speaking in a prayer language is simple and interpretation is simple, perhaps the other gifts of the Holy Spirit operate just as easily.

Oh God, if the classical Pentecostal concept of the word of knowledge is the correct one, give me an example. The lady sitting there in the third row—what is she praying about?

I had an immediate response. *She has arthritis.*

I'm not going to suggest anything to her, I thought. *I'm going to use this gift the way I've always wished it would be used.*

I jotted down a description of the woman and noted where she sat. I wrote, "Arthritis."

When the service concluded, I invited

people forward for prayer. She did not come, so I made a second appeal. Finally, the lady came. I went to her immediately and asked her need.

"Arthritis," she said.

I was excited. This was the first time this had ever happened to me. I brought her to the platform. I asked my wife, Gloria, and the pastor to come as well. I wanted them as witnesses. I explained to the congregation what the word of knowledge was, at least what I was now convinced it was because of this experience. Then I asked the pastor, the woman, and Gloria to read the note, and we prayed.

When my wife and I returned to the hotel that night, we wondered, was it coincidental? After all, it had happened only once.

The next morning I went to an Episcopal mass with a Lutheran layman. The priest asked us to read the story of the blind man in John 9 and comment on it. The congregation divided into groups of five, and we shared our thoughts.

My Lutheran friend turned to me and commented as though he possessed the word of knowledge. He based his analysis of my situation on the incident recorded in John 9.

In the story the blind man is brought to the synagogue.

"OK, you really were blind," the Pharisees say. "We've talked to your parents. You were blind and now you can see. How did it happen?"

"I've already told you the story," he replies. "Do you want to be his disciple too?"

They become infuriated. "You're his disciple. We're the disciples of Moses. We don't understand this man who defames the Sabbath and we don't know where his power comes from."

"Isn't this a mystery?" the blind man replies. "I was blind but now I can see, and you don't know where his power comes from."

The Pharisees say, in effect, "This power comes from the devil."

Now my friend's comment was directed right at me even though there were three or four other men in the group.

"All my life when anything goes wrong, I blame it on God. But, when anything good happens, I say, 'Wasn't that a coincidence?' When anything bad would happen, I would say, 'Oh God, how in Your sovereignty could You allow this to happen to me. Why are You trying to hurt me?' But when good things happened, I wouldn't give God the credit. What I learned from this story," he said, "was that God had healed a man and they wouldn't give Him the glory."

The rest of the way home in the car, I prayed silently.

God, I'm going to give You the benefit of the doubt and say that what happened last night was a miracle. It wasn't a coincidence, it was a miracle. You actually told me that she had arthritis. Regardless of what the odds are, I am going to believe You."

That marked the beginning for me. No qualifications reserve certain saints for the bestowal of the gifts—not age, distance, time, education, nationality, or attainment of a specific level of holiness. The whole realm of the gifts is at the disposal of the Christian as the Spirit wills.

When Peter declared Jesus to be "the Christ, the Son of the living God," Jesus responded, "Blessed are you, Simon Barjonas, because flesh and blood did not reveal this to you, but My Father who is in heaven" (Matthew 16:17). Though Peter was hardly a mature Christian at the time, God spoke to him.

The key to the gifts then is not education, but the acknowledgement of complete dependence upon God.

I spent my senior year in high school at Canyonville Bible Academy in Oregon. During the Thanksgiving weekend of 1963, I visited First Assembly of God Church in Portland. The guest speaker, Bob Tattenger, superintendent of the Canadian Assemblies, attracted me by his articulate delivery. Though he was young, he held the attention of that great audience. I liked it. I identified with him. Then a definite impression came to me: *You're going to preach. Some day you're going to preach in this very church just as he's doing.*

Eight years later, I was booked to speak at First Assembly, Portland, Oregon. When I walked out on the platform of the auditorium, I felt a tremendous excitement, a deep confidence. "I'm in God's will," I said.

The same thing happened to Moses. When God spoke to him from the burning bush, He said, "Certainly I will be with you, and this shall be the sign to you that it is I who have sent you: when you have brought the people out of Egypt, you shall worship God here at this mountain" (Exodus 3:12). Many years and trials later, it happened.

What amazed me was that God knew all along that I was going to be in Portland at that very church. In a moment of openness to the Lord, this impression had been given me. That gives me confidence today. I know that God is behind everything that happens to me. He is watching and knows exactly where I am and where I will be, bringing me into His perfect will. That weekend years before was perhaps the first time the word of knowledge worked for me, but I was not conscious of it as a gift until years later. I certainly do not have all of the gifts, but I am convinced that all of the gifts may be exercised by one person. It is not necessary to be more spiritual, but to be more expectant and available to God.

In 1972 I published a booklet on the word of knowledge which emphasized that very principle. Some of the 20,000 people who bought the booklet opened their own lives to gifts of revelation with amazing results.

Pastor Ken Marquis is one. After reading the booklet one evening, he asked God, "Oh Lord, if you can use Doug Wead that way, why can't you use me?"

Marquis could not go to sleep that night. While in bed, he asked God a more specific question: "If there's something about my worship service tomorrow that I should know as the pastor, tell me."

There was no answer.

Then suddenly a thought came to him, *There will be a woman in a red coat who will sit in the last row. Pray for her.*

Marquis considered it only a few seconds before rolling over in disgust at his absurd train of thought.

The next Sunday morning, a woman dressed in a red coat sat in the last row. Marquis had never seen her before. He tried to shake the impression of the previous night but he couldn't. Finally, convinced that it was more than coincidental, he acted.

"The woman in the last row in the red coat. You've been having some big problems lately and God told me to pray for you," he said.

Immediately the woman burst into tears. Marquis was surprised. Before the day was over he was able to minister to her effectively.

David Womersley, a pastor in McMinnville, Oregon, had a similar experience. He was visiting the Melodyland Christian Center in Anaheim, California. Being miles away from home, he thought it would be a good chance for him to test the availability of the gift of the word of knowledge.

One evening while attending the sessions at the center, the Holy Spirit began to speak to him about a young lady seated across from him: *She has been abused sexually by a man in her life. I want to heal her emotions and help her to forget.*

Womersley, inexperienced in such matters, found a nearby woman counselor, Sally Holiday, and told her about his impressions. Nothing happened until later in the evening when the young lady herself approached Mrs. Holiday to tell her about her troubles.

"Why, the Lord has already told that man all about your problem," the astonished Mrs. Holiday said, pointing to Womersley. Womersley was as surprised as anyone else. It was his first experience with a gift which he would often use in his pastoral ministry.

We must remember that God Himself works supernaturally through us. It is true that there are human mechanics for each of the gifts. If we want a gift of a prayer language, for example, we must participate. God will not pump the air in and out of our lungs. He will not move our tongues. We have to actually speak; He will provide the utterance and anointing. To receive the word of knowledge we must be sensitive to the Holy Spirit, and when an impression comes we must be obedient. God effects the actual miracle.

8

The Human Element

In 1973 I was involved in a conference in Livonia, Michigan, a Detroit suburb. Pastor Jacob Traub, the conference host, walked out onto the platform leaving me behind in his office. As I was praying for the evening session, the voice of the Spirit began to speak to me: *Pray for a young man. He lives in California. His mother will walk into the service late tonight. She will sit on the fifth row. She will be wearing a dark blue coat.*

That was all.

I wrote the details on paper and put them in a Bible which I left in the pastor's office. Then I went out and started the meeting.

Midway through the workshop, a woman in a dark blue coat entered the sanctuary. She hesitated for a moment, then walked down the outside aisle to a seat on the fifth row.

This time I decided not to hurry into anything. If the Lord had spoken to me prior to the service, He would speak again and tell me what He wanted me to do about the woman.

That evening there were many people who wanted personal prayer for forgiveness of sin, healing, or solutions to marital problems. I invited all those with special needs to come to the altar and to bring their Bibles with them.

We sang a few choruses, then I asked them all to find Matthew 18:20 in their Bibles, a verse I had used many times in similar situations.

I assigned various people to read the verse, "Where two or three have gathered together in My name, there I am in their midst." No one seemed to react; they all looked to me for further instruction.

"I believe that Jesus is really here," I said. "I believe that He is God. He is omnipotent. He is also omniscient; He knows everything about us."

Then the Holy Spirit directed me to call

for the woman in the dark blue coat.

She came to the platform and with a little encouragement told us the story of her son in California.

I said that the Lord already had spoken to me about her son and that the Holy Spirit was now beginning the work that would bring him to God. Then I sent her to the pastor's office to bring back the big Bible.

When I read the note to the audience and they realized that God had spoken to me about her beforehand, a few people began to cry out to God; others began to weep.

The Spirit spoke to me, *Why are they so impressed by the note?*

Then I realized a potential danger of such gifts of revelation. As these gifts become more common in the charismatic prayer groups, people may begin to look to the prophets for leadership. These prophets may begin to upstage the ultimate revelation, the Holy Scriptures. Such things had occurred in the short Pentecostal history. Now that gifts are being experienced on such a wide scale, this danger has no doubt resurfaced.

"Why are you impressed by this?" I asked, holding up the flimsy piece of paper on which I had scratched my note.

"Why are we so inspired all of a sudden? Anyone can use the gifts of the Holy

Spirit. You do not have to be special. They operate very easily."

I picked up the Bible which was opened to Matthew 18:20. "What about this? Isn't it true? Aren't these words of Jesus true which we read tonight? Why didn't these words impress us? Let's read them again."

We started reading, "Where two or three have gathered together in My name, there I am in their midst."

This time we all believed it. The words were true; we knew that Jesus was with us. We were reminded that the gifts of the Spirit can provide temporary victories, but their operation is based on the Word of God.

I think people can better understand gifts of revelation if they realize the human element involved. Not every prophecy is of God, of course. The Scriptures encourage people to test prophecies and to pass judgment on them. "Try the spirits to see whether they are from God" (1 John 4:1).

We should not be "closed" to any revelation but neither should we be too gullible. The prophecy should be tested, no matter who gives a word of knowledge.

On one occasion a pastor friend came to me in frustration. He had attended a conference, and the speaker had called him out of the audience.

"You are a pastor," the speaker told him, "and within three months you will be leaving the church you are in now and move south."

The story bothered me too. Several months later I asked someone associated with this particular speaker to explain the situation.

"Well," he said, "if the pastor didn't move south, my friend may have been in the flesh. It wasn't the Holy Spirit speaking after all. It could have been his imagination."

"Why would he take such a risk?" I asked. "Why would he say it unless he was sure it was really the Spirit of God?"

"Because you must be obedient," my friend answered. "He thought that God had spoken to him so he had to be obedient to that voice."

The emphasis is on "obedience." Be obedient to what the Spirit says to you regardless of its impact on the audience or the people involved. This has a strong scriptural precedent and explains I Kings 13, a mysterious chapter to many theologians.

My own approach has an equally important emphasis. I remain extremely sensitive to the audience. I do not expect them to accept anything that is too vague; they can challenge what I say. I am very concerned that my word of knowledge be accurate since I am declaring that God has spoken to me. Consequently, I may fail to share what the Spirit is wanting to say because I am too cautious and do not say anything.

But on some occasions I have not been cautious enough.

Before a workshop at Evangelistic Temple in Houston, Texas, I was meditating quietly in the prayer room. The Spirit instructed me to pray for someone named Helen. I made a note to that effect in my Bible, adding the date. I forgot the whole thing, and my Bible was so marked up that the little note was lost among other notes.

Five months later I held a conference in Poulsbo, Washington. While praying prior to an evening workshop, I had a distinct impression that a woman named Helen would be at the workshop, and that God in His sovereignty had brought her there for a specific reason. I was to pray for her. Then I remembered the notation in my Bible.

Is she the Helen I prayed for months ago in Houston? I wondered.

Yes, she is, came the answer.

At that point, I was confused. I was not

exactly sure what my impression was—she would be wearing either a pink coat or a pink dress. I wrote my message on paper."She will be wearing a pink coat."

A woman named Helen attended the workshop that night. She had been praying about a special problem for several months. She responded when I called for her, but there was one confusing complication. She was wearing a pink dress; her coat was another color. I apologized for the mistake and prayed for her anyway.

While errors of this kind may seem perfectly normal to the parapsychologist, it poses a problem for the theologian. Scriptural evidence argues that such mistakes should not happen if a gift is genuinely of God.

Many factors are involved. For example, there is the possibility that I misinterpreted the impression which I received from the Holy Spirit. Perhaps my own imagination confused what He was saying. But mistakes are made, and even persons with the most dramatic prophetic gifts have made mistakes.

No individual is infallible. A prophecy or word of knowledge should be challenged and judged.

The most dramatic mistake I made in

using a word of knowledge occurred during a seminar in Dallas, Texas. I arrived at the church early to pray. The workshop, with questions and answers from the audience, was to be conducted in a cafeteria in the church basement.

I arrived at the church cafeteria to pray and as I was praying, I wandered around the room. As I passed one of the tables near the front, I began to receive a message. In my mind I saw a girl sitting at the table; I knew her name. The word *cancer* came to my mind. As is my practice, I wrote the details on paper.

That night a girl did sit at that table. Her name was the same as the one given to me two hours before. But that is where the similarity ended. She did not have cancer, neither did any of her friends, neighbors, or relatives. The parents were clearly troubled by the event. I tried to reassure them by explaining that anything involving human judgment is subject to error. The situation was complicated since prophetic gifts had been in operation throughout the week and had always been accurate.

When I returned to the same church a year later, I saw that the family was still enthusiastically involved. I gave a sigh of relief. They had managed to accept the event as a mistake rather than become disillusioned altogether.

Four years later as this book was going to press, I learned that cancer did eventually occur in the Moore family. It was successfully treated. My most dramatic "mistake" was not a mistake at all.

Fear of failure is undoubtedly the major reason why many Christians have not developed gifts of revelation. They are unable or unwilling to experiment in such an area.

If God is sovereign, if He is actually in control, it is not inconceivable that He can use even human mistakes to work His will. In fact, sometimes I suspect He delights in watching me grope frantically for the right words, knowing all along that His will is not going to be subverted by my mistake.

In June 1974 I was invited to Houston, Texas, by Women's Aglow Fellowship. During an evening banquet, I began to receive impressions about a young lady: *Her husband can't keep a job and it has been very frustrating for her.*

I was about to be introduced so I didn't have much time to consider my impression. I simply wrote on paper a description of the woman and these words, "Job situation. Pray for husband."

I thought that the situation might be

embarrassing for the woman, so rather than make any mention of it publicly, I went to the woman I identified after the service.

"Are you praying about a job situation?" I asked.

She was a Roman Catholic attending her first charismatic gathering of any kind. She looked around at her friends and smiled, "Why, yes, I was just talking with them about it. We've had some problems at work."

"Are you married?" I asked.

"No."

I momentarily panicked. Since I was wrong I decided to tell her the truth—what my impression had been, that I was still learning how to use the gifts of the Holy Spirit and that obviously I had made a mistake.

"I'll have to explain this," I said, "but I wrote these impressions when I saw you earlier tonight."

I handed her the note and waited for her reaction. *She will think that I'm crazy, I thought. I will have to stand here humiliated, taking it all in. I am sure I will learn something and the experience might even be good for my pride.*

"Look at this," she laughed, showing the note to her friends. "Maybe the Lord will answer his prayer and give me a husband." They talked excitedly several minutes before I realized that they were not mocking me.

I took the note back to have another look.

"I've been praying too that I'll meet the right man," she said.

I read my note again, "Job situation. Pray for husband."

It is true that a prophet does not always realize how his prophecies will be fulfilled. God may fulfill the very words he has said but not always in the way that the prophet had in mind. Many of the songs of David were prophecies about the Messiah though the Scriptures never indicate that David himself was aware of the extent of his prophecies.

In November 1971 I held a conference in Poplar Bluff, Missouri. One evening before the service, the Spirit spoke to me while I was praying in the prayer room. *There is someone in the audience who will be sitting on your right side. She is dressed in blue. She has tumors. I will heal her. Call her out of the audience.* I wrote the message down on paper and laid it on the window sill of the prayer room.

Out on the platform, I looked to my right, searching for the woman in blue. There were a dozen.

At the conclusion of the service, I called for someone in the audience who had tumors. It was an extremely awkward time because no one responded for seven or eight minutes. That's a long time for no activity in a public meeting. Finally a man responded and I prayed for him and left a little discouraged.

When the service was over, the pastor's wife called to me in the lobby. "Did you have anyone in particular in mind when you asked to pray for someone who had tumors?" she asked.

I really did not want to discuss my own personal spiritual experiences with her and sheepishly answered in the negative.

"Well, the lady sitting next to me has tumors, but she has been prayed for so many times that I'm sure she was embarrassed and reluctant to respond."

"What was the lady wearing?" I asked.

"A blue dress."

I ran back into the prayer room, grabbed my note and showed it to the pastor's wife. She was amazed and so was I.

People do not always respond to the word of knowledge, or for some reason or another, they forfeit what could have been a miracle.

As you begin to allow the Holy Spirit to operate the gifts through you, don't be inhibited by fear of error. All beginners make mistakes, though the gifts are perfect for they are of God. If the gifts are manifested in love and humility, they may be exercised without fear for edification to the Body of Christ.

9

Before You Begin

I have drawn four conclusions from my years of experimentation with the word of knowledge.

First, it is one of the gifts of the Holy Spirit.

Debate will continue over which of the nine gifts it actually is. Some will maintain that it should be categorized as a part of the gift of prophecy; others will believe that it is a working of miracles. Regardless, this ability to receive information through extrasensory means was a gift which operated in the New

Testament Church as a gift of the Holy Spirit.

This does not rule out the fact that there is an evil counterpart to this God-given gift. Even if the spiritual condition of a person is corrupt and his motivation is wrong, he can achieve similar results. In this case, the ability to operate the gift comes from an evil source and the extrasensory perception is satanic.

In concluding that the word of knowledge is a gift of the Holy Spirit, I do not rule out the fact that there are aspects of its operation which may be explained in scientific terms. The point is that Jesus operated the gift with perfection. You too, without understanding completely how it operates, can receive this free gift from God.

Second, I have concluded that the successful operation of this gift involves human participation.

The voice of the Spirit will not overwhelm a person. When the kings of Judah and Israel consulted with Elisha concerning their war plans, the prophet made a strange request. He asked for someone to play the lute. While he was relaxed and listening to the music, the Lord spoke to him. Elisha had evidently learned that he must be in the right frame of mind in order to receive God's instructions.

The Holy Spirit may speak to you even though you have not asked Him to speak. Alexander Solzhenitsyn in *Gulag Archipelago* talks about an ability to spot an informer among the other prisoners in Russian labor camps. This "sensor relay" as he calls it, worked perfectly. Corrie ten Boom in her best-seller, *The Hiding Place*, also records many moments when she intuitively knew what to do to escape the Gestapo.

I believe an individual hears the voice of God in these emergency moments. He is desperate and he is utterly dependent on God. He becomes willing to believe.

I am convinced that if an individual will listen closely, he can hear the voice of God even in an ordinary situation. He can let such impressions give him ideas or encouragement. He does not have to abandon common sense, but by checking out an impression he may discover that it actually was God who led him. Perhaps the Holy Spirit will lead him to the right place or prompt him to say the very words that bring hope to someone who desperately needs them.

Most Christians imagine that God occasionally leads them in such a manner. I contend that this relationship can be developed until a highly sophisticated gift emerges. Its value for counseling, evangelism, and loving other people is obvious. However, this gift will not automatically develop just because one believes in it; one must receive it, participate, experiment and try.

Third, I have concluded that the operation of the gift of the word of knowledge is not infallible, for the very reason that it involves human participation. It is possible for the most sincere and gifted Christian to give a word of knowledge in good faith and still to be mistaken. Some will suggest, referring to Deuteronomy 18:21-22, that if an individual makes one mistake, he is therefore not a prophet. But if the gift is not a prophetic gift but rather the word of knowledge; the Deuteronomy criteria need not apply.

Yet the question arises: if these are God-given gifts, why hasn't God given us the ability to use them perfectly? Why should there ever be mistakes? This question is similar to: why isn't everyone healed? An answer is that God doesn't want us to have an unhealthy dependence on His gifts. It is possible for one to become corrupted by God's own blessings.

Imagine you are a wealthy and powerful man. You love your son and he knows that if he's ever in trouble he can count on you. But if you don't discipline yourself, you may corrupt him by your money and power. He may fail to develop responsibility; he may never learn to work for himself. So even though you have more than enough money, you make sure he learns to be independent and resourceful.

God does heal sick bodies, but He also expects us to eat the right foods, get sufficient sleep, and give our minds a chance for diversion and relaxation. Why should God use His gifts to endorse our abuses and sins?

If gifts of revelation were not special occurrences, we could develop lazy habits. There would be no place for Bible study and research. God would do all the thinking for us. We would lose the capacity to reason which makes us unique as humans.

Finally, I have one last observation on the gift of the word of knowledge: it must be operated in faith. Once a person develops a healthy appreciation for the limits of a gift of revelation, he is then in a position to develop it. However, the word of knowledge will have no effect unless the person operating it has the confidence that God can use such a procedure.

Most doctors agree that the majority of their patients have problems that are psychosomatic in origin. Some doctors have discovered with amazement the power of suggestion. They will tell a patient that his condition will last three days, and sure enough, three days later the patient begins to feel better. Doctors who give evasive and uncertain answers are surprised to see inconsistent results. Most doctors develop a confident and commanding air because they have discovered that their attitudes can be part of the healing process.

If a Christian fails to accept the fact that he can make mistakes, this kind of confidence can be devastating. However, if he is humble before God and does not rule over people, he can use a word of knowledge with faith to make a powerful impact on a life.

I have been on the receiving end of this activity only four times. On two occasions the word given to me was absolutely wrong. I didn't act on it, of course. But I will never forget one occasion when a person addressed some very personal needs deep within me. He was very kind; very sure of himself. And he was incredibly accurate. It had a dramatic, practical spiritual effect on my life. It was not an emotional moment for me. The key to its success was the self-confidence of the person who gave me the word of knowledge.

After you have become acquainted with the simple human mechanics of this gift, after you have accepted the fact that you will never be infallible (in this life anyway), you must begin the building process. You must build the faith to believe that God can speak to man through such a simple conduit as man himself. You must believe that God can speak to man in spite of man's weakness.

With these facts in mind, here are some simple steps to initiate the word of knowledge.

First, ask God for His anointing on your life and explain to Him that you do not despise His choice of gifts. Tell Him that you would welcome the word of knowledge if it were His will to give it to you. Tell Him that you repent of any pride that may have kept you from opening your life to such a possibility.

Second, learn to spot occasions when information is needed. Choose a moment when you could be of great help to a person if you knew more about his situation. Instead of prying, ask God to show you his needs.

Then, listen for the voice of God. If you receive an impression, do not be too quick to dismiss it. Consider it.

Next, confront the person with your impression. Do this very humbly and slowly. "As we were praying together, I felt concerned for your family. Would you want me to pray a blessing on your marriage?"

If the response is positive, you can pursue it. "I felt as though your wife has hurt you deeply. If this is true, let us pray for her and for a healing in your life."

If it appears that you are wrong, do not apologize too quickly. Persons are very reluctant to open up their lives to someone else. They may deny what you say even though they know you are right.

However, it would be foolish to heap condemnation on them by striking out at them, "You know it is true!" Besides, you are not infallible, and you may be wrong.

One point of caution here. Do not conclude from one experience or even one dozen experiences that you cannot use such a gift. The word of knowledge, like speaking in tongues, may operate in some individuals only after many months of prayer, study, and experimentation. Remain open to the fact that God can speak to you.

This raises some troubling questions. How can one be sure that it is the Holy Spirit who is giving him the impression? What if a person receives conflicting impressions? These are questions I will address in Part III, "The Ministry of the Word of Knowledge."

Part III

Ministry of
the Word
of Knowledge

10

The Voice of
the Spirit and Healing

People can more easily believe that God will help them when they are sure He really knows how badly they hurt. The Holy Spirit often will use the word of knowledge to let people know He is aware of a situation and to stimulate their faith for divine healing. Kathryn Kuhlman's ministry dramatically illustrated this as did William Branham's ministry in the 1950s.

During a week in Kelso, Washington, my wife and I became good friends with associate pastor Larry Dublanko and his wife, Sharon. One evening their baby became quite ill. He was vomiting and running a high fever. We all were worried. Sharon telephoned their doctor who arranged an appointment for the following morning.

Larry and I walked over to the nearby sanctuary where a seminar was about to begin. I left Larry and went into a small room near the church offices to pray. As I was praying, I began to receive an impression.

Tonight Larry is going to lead the song service. He will be leading the song "Whosoever Meaneth Me." When he does, stop him!

I immediately fought this impression; it was just too absurd. Once a favorite of fundamentalist congregations, this song had all but disappeared in evangelistic worship and I hadn't heard it for many years.

But the impression persisted. I considered how mysteriously God's gifts had operated in the past. *I can't make anything happen,* I prayed. *If this is really You, God, why would You want me to do this?*

Once again the impression came, *Stop him! I am going to heal his son!* I wrote the message in my Bible.

But pastor Don Mallough decided to lead the congregational singing himself that evening. He met Larry in the hall before going into the sanctuary.

"I have some choruses selected," Larry said. "I thought it would be better than singing from the hymnal."

"Well, actually, I thought I'd lead the singing tonight," Mallough answered.

"All right," Larry said.

Mullough hesitated. "But since you have some choruses ready, why don't you go ahead with them?"

Larry Dublanko led three choruses. As the congregation finished the last line of "The Windows of Heaven," he announced, "Page 262 in the hymnal." Later he said that he wasn't even sure it was the right page for the tune he wanted.

The congregation sang the first line, "I am happy today and the sun shines bright" before I finally found the page. We were singing "Whosoever Meaneth Me." It was a difficult moment as I interrupted the service. Larry was flabbergasted. I showed him my note, and then sent him to his adjacent apartment to pray for his little son, Craig.

Craig was healed! He woke up the next morning laughing in his crib. His swollen eyes were back to normal; his cough and fever were gone.

God used this word of knowledge to build our faith that He would heal Craig.

In October 1973 I flew to Phoenix, Arizona. That night in the city, a Nazarene couple contacted me. "What is a charismatic seminar?" they asked. "Will there be prayer for the sick?"

I assured them that there would be prayer. The couple attended each night's session. On the third night they sat near the front. At the conclusion of the service, the pastor and the deacons of the church assisted me in praying for those at the altar who wanted divine healing.

After the special prayer for healing, the couple were beaming. I was curious because they seemed to have so much confidence that something had happened to them when we prayed. They gave me a fascinating explanation for their faith.

Months before, the man and his wife had been in the congregation when the Rev. Ernest Moen, pastor, had announced an upcoming charismatic seminar. The couple were members of a Nazarene church but had been joining Moen's congregation for evening services. They knew little about the renewal movement, but each had experienced a prayer language in private devotions. The wife had been praying for a miracle of healing.

As Moen announced our upcoming seminar, the Holy Spirit began to speak to her: *You will be healed during that seminar!* The impression was so strong that she shared it with her husband and many of her friends. No one could explain it, and everyone but the man and his wife discounted it as imaginary. They waited patiently several months, confident that the simple impression was actually God's voice.

They had stumbled onto a spiritual gift that was too obvious and easy for many great theologians and leaders in the charismatic movement. I gave them a stern warning that such impressions must fit the guidelines of Scripture and that they should never rely on such impressions for guidance unless there was other practical evidence too. Yet there can be no doubt that this event had given them increased faith to believe for a miracle of healing.

We conduct a yearly seminar at Bethel Temple, the oldest Pentecostal church in Dallas, Texas, and at one time the largest Pentecostal church in the United States. One night prior to the evening service, I was praying in the pastor's office. The Holy Spirit began to speak to me about a woman in the audience: *She will be sitting on your left, wearing an orange and red* dress. *She has heart trouble.*

"What do you want me to do, Lord?" I asked.

I want you to tell her that I am the resurrection and the life. I want you to pray for her.

I wrote the words on paper. On my way out of the office, the book titled *Arena of Faith* caught my eye. Taking the book from the shelf I placed my note inside.

As I was teaching later, I suddenly saw an elderly woman seated at my left. Her dress had several different patterns of orange and red. *She is the one,* the Holy Spirit said. At the conclusion of the session, I went to her in the audience and brought her with me to the front. I asked her to explain to us what she had been praying for.

"I have a heart condition," she began, and burst into tears.

I sent her and a friend back to the pastor's office to retrieve *Arena of Faith.*

They found my note. In amazement the woman kept repeating the words I had written, "I am the resurrection and the life."

I invited the deacons to join us for a prayer. But at that point something happened which is hard to explain. I had a feeling that something was wrong, and I could see that some of the others with us, including the woman, felt it too. For a few seconds I inwardly panicked. *Don't lose your confidence now,* I thought. *Doubt is a normal thing and that's probably what it is—doubt.*

Then the Lord spoke to me, *I am going to show you something about two deacons in this church.* What the Holy Spirit showed me and what I said privately to the group on the platform is of a personal nature. Since I am using real names and locations in these reports, it would serve no constructive purpose to explain the details. After a few general comments to the pastor and deacons, we prayed for the woman.

A year later I was at Bethel Temple in Dallas again.

"I just got a telephone call," the pastor said. "Remember that woman with the serious heart condition you prayed for last year?"

I nodded.

"But do you remember what you said about two of the deacons when we started to pray together for that woman last year?"

"Yes."

"Well, I didn't know exactly what you were talking about that night but you were on the right track," he said. "Someday I'll tell you about it. Two of the men are no longer members of this church."

During a seminar at the Neighborhood Christian Church in Canby, Oregon, the Holy Spirit showed me what would happen at the conclusion of my teaching. In my mind I saw a small group of people walk to the front of the sanctuary for special prayer.

Count them, the Holy Spirit said.

I counted eleven people.

At the end of the lesson on faith, the service unfolded exactly as I had seen it in my mind. I shared what the Holy Spirit had shown me and a note which I had written to that effect.

"God knew that each of us would stand here for prayer tonight," I said. "I do not believe that God would bring us to this moment without an important reason. Some of you will receive a miracle."

One of the women, Mrs. Hazel Rydz, began to weep. She was trying to have faith that God would heal her of diabetes. Pastor Ken Marquis and I laid hands on her for prayer. Later she said that she began to feel a warm sensation at that moment, and knew she was being healed.

Yet that Sunday night, Mrs. Rydz became violently ill. The following day she continued to feel nauseated. Finally, she made an appointment with her doctor in Oregon City. On Tuesday evening, Hazel Rydz stood before the audience so happy that she could hardly speak. The doctor had run tests and had found that her blood sugar was at a normal level.

"I can't understand it," he said.

What had happened was that Sunday night her body had begun to react to the insulin which she no longer needed. Tuesday afternoon the doctor began the process of taking her off the insulin. That night she was able to stand before the audience with a radiant smile.

"God has healed me," she said. "I never believed that it could happen. It's like a dream."

Pat Robertson, author of *Shout It on the Housetops*, and founder of the Christian Broadcasting Network, has his own religious telecast which is seen nightly in some of the largest cities of the U.S. Robertson, a Baptist, is deeply involved in the charismatic movement and openly uses the word of knowledge on his television program. Some of his critics believe that it is extrasensory perception and not a spiritual gift at all. Others say that his television audience is so vast that he could not miss with his prophetic claims. Yet the abundance of mail which daily pours into the CBN headquarters illustrates the dramatic effect his faith has on his viewers and other people.

Robertson relates this incident: "As we were praying God showed me that there was a person whose right forearm had been broken and was in a cast. God was healing it. As I was leaving the studio at the end of the program, I was approached by two women in their middle years. The older of the two had her forearm in a cast. When I saw her, I was asked to pray for them. I replied, 'The work has already been done.'

"They thought I had some special revelation at that time, but this was not the case. This woman had actually been healed when the word was given to me. But the miracle was that neither she nor her friend were listening or watching the broadcast when it occurred. They were not aware that there had been such a word during the program only about thirty minutes previously. Two days later she returned to her doctor who X-rayed the break. He found that almost two inches of bone had grown in the arm where the bone previously had been completely crushed. The bone was joined together and he was able to remove the cast."

Robertson's faith also reached the Don Van Scoy family of Farmers Branch, Texas. Don relates, "When my son Doug was four years old, his eyes became severely crossed. We took him for an eye examination shortly afterwards and the doctor said he had to wear corrective glasses. The glasses helped his vision, but if he went without them for any length of time, his eyes would begin to cross again. It was no small job keeping a boy that age in glasses, and the glasses were not cheap.

"Shortly before the healing occurred, we had taken him for another eye examination. His vision was good but the doctor said that he should still wear the glasses because his eye muscles were weak and still needed help. He said that he might recommend surgery when Doug was sixteen or seventeen, but that nothing could be done now.

"One day last spring, our whole family was at home watching the '700 Club,' a television program on the Christian Broadcasting Network. As we watched we also prayed over Doug at different times as we were directed to by the leader of the program. In addition to the crossed eyes, we were also praying for sores which had developed on his gums. After the program had gone on for awhile, Doug went outside to shoot some baskets out by the garage.

Shortly after he left, the man leading the program said he felt that someone was being healed of crossed eyes and sores of the mouth. When Doug came back in, my wife asked him about the sores in his mouth.

" 'I can hardly feel them,' he said. 'I can tell they're going away.'

"Then my wife said, 'Why don't you take off your glasses, too?'

"He did, and said, 'I can see better without my glasses than with them.'

"So we said, 'Just leave them off for awhile and see how your eyes do.'

"That was a year ago. Doug hasn't had to wear glasses since then, and his eyes have been straight, not crossed .... How great is the Lord."

In February 1974 my wife and I were invited to Olympia, Washington, to hold a seminar for pastor Glen Cole at Evergreen Christian Center. Our first service was held on Sunday morning. Perhaps 60 percent of the audience was thirty years old or younger. As I walked onto the platform and relaxed in a plush chair, I noticed an elderly lady with silver-gray hair. In my mind, I saw Jesus standing beside her with one hand on her shoulder.

I prayed, *Who is she, Lord?* Then I felt a very strong impression: *She has cancer.*

Something else caught my attention just then and I forgot about the woman.

In the evening service, I noticed her again. The Lord again spoke to me about her, *She is praying about a fear of cancer.*

This time the impression was so strong that I decided to write it down. I wrote, "Woman on third row, blue dress, gray hair, center section, cancer? Begin to pray for her."

As I wrote the last sentence, the Holy Spirit said, *No! I want you to begin to believe for her healing.*

The Holy Spirit also showed me what would happen at the altar that evening. He showed me people coming with various needs. When I saw them standing at the altar, He told me to count them. I counted twenty-two. But, I thought, *twenty-two people aren't very many for a crowd this size.* The Holy Spirit showed me that the twenty-two would respond first and they would be a sign to build other people's faith. So I wrote down his message to me, "Twenty-two will respond—and also, invite the pastors." I put the note into my Bible.

At the conclusion of the service, I gave an altar call for anyone with a special need. Slowly they began to come down.

Seventeen, eighteen, nineteen and no more. I waited a moment longer, then invited the pastors. Pastor Glen Cole and his two associates joined me at the altar. There were now twenty-two people standing, just as I had seen.

I thought to myself, *Well, God, this really must be You.* I pulled the note from my Bible and asked the pastor to read it aloud. He read, "There will be twenty-two—invite the pastors."

Then I noticed the lady with the silver-gray hair—about whom the Lord had spoken to me that morning. She was standing among the twenty-two. She later identified herself as Wanda McKay, a Roman Catholic who had started attending services at Evergreen Christian Center three months previously. She had heard about the charismatic movement and had felt a need for a closer relationship with Christ.

"You're praying for a miracle, aren't you?" I asked her.

"Yes, I have a brain tumor."

"Cancer," I said softly, remembering my note and what the Lord had told me about her.

"Yes," she answered.

Moments later we were standing before hundreds of people asking God to heal her. Wanda read my note and I explained to her what had happened. But before we prayed I called to the audience, "Who will look up Matthew 18:20?"

Many responded so I asked all of them to stand and one by one read it aloud. Scattered throughout the entire congregation, they read, "Where two or three of you have gathered together in my name, there I am in their midst."

"Wanda, do you believe that Jesus is here?" I asked.

"Yes, I do," she said.

I reminded the audience that we can't *make* God do anything, but that Jesus told us to ask and we shall receive. Then I turned to Mrs. McKay. "Just ask Jesus for whatever you want."

"Jesus, help me. I'm sick." Wanda's voice quavered.

"Wanda," I asked, "do you believe that when we anoint you with oil, Jesus will heal you?"

"Yes."

The pastor and his associates joined me as we laid hands on Wanda McKay.

"In the name of Jesus, be healed," Pastor Cole said authoritatively.

By now many other people had come to the front. Ten minutes later I saw Mrs. McKay in the crowd once again. Trying to get my attention, she had a beaming smile on her face.

"The pressure is gone," she said when we were near enough to talk.

It is true that the operation of the word of knowledge doesn't necessarily guarantee healing. But God's will is complex and so many factors are involved in a healing that it is hard to pinpoint the role which the word of knowledge plays. The point is that such a manifestation of the Holy Spirit often accompanies the gift of healing.

After an evening seminar in Houston, Texas, Ernie Fridge was with a group of people discussing what had happened.

"How did the Holy Spirit show the speaker details about other people?" someone asked.

"I don't know," Fridge answered, "but remember Vera Smith? When Doug Wead was here two years ago, he called her out of the audience and told her what was wrong with her. Nothing ever came of it."

Coincidentally, that night the Rev. Robert Way, pastor, had asked Vera Smith to give a testimony.

"Two years ago, Doug Wead conducted a seminar here in Houston," she began. "He said that there was someone in the audience who had pains in her chest. Well, as most of you know, I never respond to altar appeals, but since he came to me and took me out of the audience, I went with him."

Vera Smith had been suffering from a hiatus hernia. She was prayed for that night. Her chest pains ceased and occasionally Vera would comment to friends, "I believe the Lord has healed me." But how could anyone really know?

A week before I returned to Houston the second time, Vera Smith began to experience chest pains again. She went to the doctor who had diagnosed the hiatus hernia. He telephoned the next day to say that his X-rays showed no hernia, neither did a complete upper gastrointestinal series. The hiatus hernia was gone. The chest pains were caused by something else.

When I arrived in Houston, Vera determined to tell her church what had happened. After her testimony, Ernie Fridge stood up and told everyone about his afternoon conversation. We all had a good laugh, then paused for a moment to consider the fact that God really does heal. Two years before, the same congregation had witnessed a miracle of healing. Only now we were discovering that fact.

In 1976 I returned to Olympia and heard Wanda McKay testify to the fact that the cancer had completely disappeared from her body.

11

The Voice of
the Spirit and Comfort

Winston Churchill once said that the mind can stand anything except a mystery. News, whether it is good or bad, comes as a relief to a person in a crisis situation.

Perhaps the greatest benefit of the word of knowledge is the encouragement it can bring to individuals. Even if no accompanying promise or prophecy indicates that the crisis will end, the assurance that God knows about a situation encourages the heart and destroys some of the anxiety.

God comforted the Old Testament

prophet Elijah when he fled from Queen Jezebel's threats on his life (I Kings 19). He left his servant at Beersheba, the last outpost of civilization, and went alone into the wilderness. After traveling all day, he collapsed under a juniper tree and asked God to let him die. He slept and God awakened him hours later to a great supernaturally prepared meal.

God called Elijah farther into the wilderness so he left his miraculous oasis and struggled for forty days to Mount Horeb. There he lived in a cave, feeling he was the only man in the kingdom who did not worship the heathen god Baal.

During this time of discouragement, God visited the old prophet. A great windstorm sent rocks hurling down the mountains but, the Bible says, God was not in the wind. After the wind came an earthquake, but God was not in the earthquake. Neither was He in the fire. Only a gentle breeze, a whisper, carried God's voice to Elijah.

God gave Elijah detailed instructions on how he was to influence the corrupted governments of Israel and Syria. He told him to anoint Elisha as a prophet to follow him. Then He said, "incidentally, there are seven thousand men in Israel who have never bowed to Baal."

These last words shook Elijah deeply.

He shed his self-pity and doubt, and returned to challenge the evil governments of Queen Jezebel of Samaria and King Benhadad of Damascus. Elijah had no Gallup Poll to assure him that there was a nucleus of support for his anti-government activities, but through the word of knowledge he knew that seven thousand other people were faithful followers of Jehovah God. When the old prophet returned from the wilderness, he was bold and outspoken. His fearless challenge to the crimes of the government eventually began a revolution that swept Israel and Syria.

I have seen the word of knowledge operate in a similar way, encouraging people and bringing comfort to them in the midst of crisis, but without forcing them into decisions.

In 1973 I spent two weeks in ministry to prayer groups and churches in Baton Rouge, Louisiana. The Rev. Ron Wood, a pastor and talented writer in the city, had arranged the two weeks, announcing them as "Days of Christian Renewal." During the second week there were numerous reports of people who had experienced Christ, also of many gifts of the Holy Spirit in operation.

Mr. and Mrs. Guy Tanner, Presbyterians living in suburban Baton Rouge, were going through a time of great frustration. A young man had lived with them for some time as a foster child and now, as a result of many legal complications, was to be assigned a new home by the courts.

One day Beth Tanner set aside all her work to pray and fast, asking God for the assurance that the young man whom they loved so much would be given a Christian home. Of course, there would be no way of knowing since the courts could not reveal any information.

Later that evening I sat in Pastor Ron Wood's study waiting for the evening seminar to begin. I had just read several chapters from the book of Acts, amazed by the faith of the New Testament Christians. Then the Holy Spirit began to tell me about a lady who would walk into the service late. She would sit on the seventh row from the back on my left-hand side and she would be wearing a beige dress. I was to call her out of the audience and pray for her—there was no other information.

When I walked out onto the platform, I looked to the left and counted seven rows from the back. A few seats were available on the row, but there wasn't a woman in the building wearing a beige dress.

In the middle of my sermon, a couple

came in and walked slowly down the aisle; they chose the seventh row. The woman took off her coat. She was wearing a beige dress.

I called her to the front of the sanctuary for a special prayer almost immediately. I had never seen her or her husband; I didn't know why I was praying for her. Yet the words that I spoke were as accurate as though the script had been written by God.

"Here is a woman whom God hears," I said to the audience. "When this woman prays, God listens. If you are ever in trouble and want someone to pray for you, call on this woman!"

Beth Tanner stood there in tears. She believed that God is all-powerful and that He had heard her prayers. Though Mr. and Mrs. Tanner may never see the young man to whom they gave so much of their love and faith, they are confident that he is in God's hands.

A remarkable experience occurred during a chapel service at Trinity College in Ellendale, North Dakota.

Mike Waldner, a ministerial student, was going through a crisis. He had come to Trinity College with a desire to some day be a pastor, but as the school year wore on,

Mike began to doubt his calling.

He recalls, "I remember one afternoon making a note in my ministerial relations book, 'Am I really called into the ministry?' My heart was in it, but still I wasn't sure. My father was a carpenter and his father before him. Carpentry was something I understood."

During this time of self-examination, Mike was scheduled to deliver a sermon to the entire chapel. He prayed about it and still was quite confused. He considered canceling his appointment.

I arrived at Trinity in November 1974. Early one morning I was awakened by a telephone call. I cannot even remember the substance of my conversation, but after putting the receiver down I began to think about what I was planning to teach the students in chapel later that morning.

What then occurred can only be described as a vision. In my mind I saw a young man. He was seated at the very end of the row in a large audience. He was wearing glasses and he was dressed in brown.

Anoint him, the Holy Spirit said to me. In my vision I invited several of the teachers and ministers to join me in a special prayer of ordination for the young man.

Two hours later it actually happened.

At chapel, Mike Waldner walked in late. There weren't any seats available, so for the first time in his student life, he went to the front row and sat down on an end seat. Waldner, wearing glasses, was dressed in brown.

"This morning the Lord showed me this young man in a vision," I told the audience. "I am going to obey the Holy Spirit and do what I feel He wants me to do. I have written instructions on paper, but I left them home in my Bible."

I turned to a nearby teacher, Mrs. Kaye Garrison, and said, "Go to the nearest office and telephone across town to my wife Gloria. Tell her to read you the notes which I left in my Bible and then come back and tell us what they say."

Mrs. Garrison started to leave.

"Take someone with you," I called out to her.

Mrs. Garrison took the hand of the nearest student. They returned moments later with a copy of the words from my notes. There was a description of Mike Waldner, where he would sit and what he would wear. "Anoint him," the note said.

The young lady who had accompanied Mrs. Garrison to the telephone was shaken pretty badly. She had heard Gloria read the note over the telephone and had copied it. What especially bothered her was that she herself had begun to pray for Mike Waldner three days before. She didn't really know why she should pray since they didn't know each other well. Yet she sensed that he was in turmoil. It was all a little too miraculous for a young Methodist. Why had Kaye Garrison selected her? At the same time she couldn't deny what was happening; she was involved.

We anointed Mike for whatever special calling God had in mind.

Several days later he stopped by the school administration offices to talk. He explained the whole story.

"You know, it's really something," he said. "You couldn't have known what I was wearing. I haven't worn brown all week." He laughed. "And I've never sat in that seat in a chapel service!"

Mike now was at peace with himself.

"Two days before, I remember walking back to the dorm from a chapel service," he said. "I prayed, 'Oh God, give me a confirmation that you want me in the ministry.' Well, now I cannot deny what has happened."

In a similar manner, God brought encouragement to a minister in Scottsdale, Arizona, who had been experiencing great financial pressures. We were in a conference in this suburb of Phoenix. One evening prior to the service, the Holy Spirit began to speak to me: *In the audience would be a minister, wearing a green suit, who was experiencing great financial pressures.* I wrote down the message and walked out onto the platform. The pastor was opening the service. He called for a visiting minister to come to the platform and pray. He was sitting next to a man in a green suit.

I leaned toward the minister who was next to me on the platform and said, "The man sitting next to you in the green suit, is he a minister too?"

"Yes," he said, "he's from Teen Challenge, a religious organization that works with drug addicts."

Now I was convinced that God had spoken to me. I handed the minister my note. "Give this to him when you go back down to your seat."

Moments later the visiting minister in the green suit was silently reading my note. He looked up from his place in the audience and nodded his head to me. Yes, he had tremendous financial pressures involving a project of the Teen Challenge operation. Almost thirty thousand dollars was needed. I called him out of the audience immediately and we prayed. God brought deep comfort and hope to him, and weeks later his project had a great success.

The Apostle Paul frequently used the word of knowledge in his ministry as an encouragement to others. While on board ship traveling to Italy, according to Acts 27, Paul was shown that the ship would be lost in a great storm at sea. The ship's captain refused to believe him at first, but Paul quietly earned such a reputation among the prisoners and guards that his unusual warning began to gain credibility. Eventually the ship encountered a terrifying storm, and everyone looked to Paul for advice.

Paul insisted that if they stayed together, everyone would live through the storm. The captain, who at first was planning to kill the prisoners and abandon ship, was encouraged by Paul's confidence. God was right about the storm so the captain decided to trust Him this time. Eleven days later the ship broke up on the rocks, but every man survived.

On numerous occasions the Holy Spirit has allowed me to encourage people who are praying for someone they love. I'll always remember one night in August 1973. Gloria and I were in Corpus Christi,

Texas, staying at a twelve-story Holiday Inn on the Gulf of Mexico. I took a long walk that evening soaking up the beauty of the water, the sunset and the sound of the sea gulls. God spoke to me about the meeting we would have that night. He wanted to do something special for someone and no matter how unimportant I thought it was, He wanted me to play my part in His plan.

Later I understood. I was speaking to a congregation which had been burned by the charismatic movement, which had found it a source of confusion and division. Yet God was speaking to me about a couple in the audience. They were praying for their son. I knew that God wanted me to talk to them and to pray with them, even though it seemed as though this would only further irritate and alienate people who already were disillusioned by an overemphasis on the gifts of the Holy Spirit.

But God knew about the situation in Corpus Christi; He had said that He wanted to do something special for someone and that I should do my part. I wrote the message down on paper and later called the couple forward for special prayer.

As it turned out, this was a great comfort to the man and wife who had been praying for their son. But it did more. Many people in the audience identified with my low-key approach to the gifts of the Holy Spirit, and the reputation of the renewal movement made a comeback in the church.

In 1974, in Salem, Oregon, a similar incident occurred. I had been invited to conduct a conference at the People's Church where Dennis Davis is pastor. I was sitting on the platform looking out into the audience when the Holy Spirit began to speak to me about various people in the audience. *That man and wife on the ninth row are praying for their son.*

I made a note of the message and wrote a description of the woman. She was wearing a red dress and a black coat.

During special prayer at the altar I went to her and asked her if she was praying for something special.

"I have a son in Washington," she said. "I'm praying that God will save him."

"I have a message for you," I answered. "God has heard your prayers and has spoken to me about your son." Then I produced my note.

I had the woman read several Scriptures to the whole congregation.

"God is in control of the situation," I

assured her, "and He will give your son every opportunity to make a decision for Christ."

The man and wife were encouraged.

I learned of an interesting sidelight to this story later in the week. The woman in the red dress was a Mrs. Wiley. For years she had been praying about her eyesight. She had strong prescription glasses but still she couldn't see well enough to read.

Usually in any prayer situation, Mrs. Wiley would pray about her eyes. That night she had forgotten about her own problem and had been thinking about her son. When I asked her to read from the Bible, people in the audience, including her own daughter, knew that she couldn't read. To everyone's astonishment Mrs. Wiley read the small print of the King James Version of the Bible quite easily.

During a conference at a classical Pentecostal church in Mattoon, Illinois, the Holy Spirit began to reveal some things to me about a man in the audience. I recorded my impressions on paper and at the conclusion of the service, I talked to him.

"God is prospering you and blessing you," I said.

"Yes," he replied.

"He is going to continue to prosper you," I told him. "He will open the windows of heaven and pour blessing on you."

The man shook his head in agreement. "God has been so good," he said. "I am earning fourteen times the income I had only a few months ago."

Then I turned to some people nearby. "Some in this church have despised this man. He has a tobacco habit. But God is going to use him in a dramatic way no matter what you think of him." I turned to the man. "And God will help you win the battle against the cigaret."

Moments such as this provide deep reassurance to the person involved. Sometimes the encouragement can be very practical as well.

During special services in Grant's Pass, Oregon, I shared the program with a popular Christian rock singing group. They traveled first class and projected great confidence.

The Holy Spirit told me that something was wrong. The group was experiencing some serious financial problems.

After I ministered, the leader of the singing group was among many people who came to the front of the sanctuary wanting prayer. I went to him first. "What's the problem?"

"It's a financial thing." He shrugged as though he didn't want to go into detail.

"Well, the Lord has spoken to me about

it," I said. Then I showed him what the Holy Spirit had told me earlier and what I had written on paper. "God is going to help you," I said.

Pastor Oliver Summers jumped into the discussion immediately. A special offering was taken for the group.

Later that evening, over a cup of coffee at a local restaurant, the young man told us the story. He and his group had been invited to sing for a statewide youth conference sponsored by a classical Pentecostal denomination. The director of the conference had agreed to pay the traveling expenses of the group and to give them a substantial honorarium. Months later it was obvious that the director was not going to give the singing group any money whatsoever.

"There was approximately four hundred dollars we were counting on. Now we have credit card expenses long overdue. I don't know what will happen."

"That's strange," said Pastor Summers with a big smile. He pulled a check out of his suitcoat pocket. "Your offering tonight was $400."

12

The Voice of
the Spirit and Prophecy

The gift of the word of knowledge has a unique relationship to the gift of prophecy. Often it is impossible to distinguish between the two. When the disciples asked Jesus where they should meet for the Passover meal, He gave them some mysterious instructions:

And He said to them, "Behold, when you have entered the city, a man will meet you carrying a pitcher of water; follow him into the house that he enters. And you shall say to the owner of the house, 'The Teacher says to you, "Where is the guest room in which I may eat the Passover with My disciples?" ' And he will show you a large, furnished, upper room; prepare it there." And they departed and found everything just as He had told them; and they prepared the Passover—Luke 22:10-13.

It is debatable whether this is an example of what is now popularly considered to be the word of knowledge or whether Jesus was prophesying when He told them that they would meet the man carrying a pitcher of water.

During a special conference in Jacksonville, Florida, a situation occurred which would be hard to categorize. While praying before the service, the Holy Spirit began to show me a young man who would be in the audience that night. In my mind's eye I could see him. He was wearing brown pants and an orange shirt; he was sitting near the aisle in the last row in the church.

"Who is the young man?" I asked God. The answer came, *He has been praying for spiritual guidance. He is an idealist, constantly trying to improve himself, yet he is out of work and he needs financial*

*help. I am going to help him. Tell him to
believe that.*

As usual, I wrote my impressions on
paper in detail.

The church was filled that night. When I
walked to the platform I glanced back to
the last row. There he was, just as the Holy
Spirit had shown me in my mind.

At the conclusion of the workshop, he
was among the nearly eighty people who
came to the altar for special prayer. I
moved through the crowd until I found
him.

"What are you praying about?"

His head was bowed. He hesitated
before saying, "I've been praying about a
spiritual problem. I want to be a better
Christian."

"What about your personal life? Is there
anything you have been praying about?"

"I need a job," he answered.

I took a microphone and explained to the
audience what had happened to me prior
to the service. I told them that I believed
that God was going to help this young man
who, by this time, was profoundly shaken.

Three days later he stood behind the
pulpit at Southside Assembly of God in
Jacksonville, Florida, to report to me, the
Rev. Dale Zink, and the congregation that
the prayer had been answered. God had
given him a job.

In 1970 Pastor Robert Carrington invited me to hold services at Bethel Temple in Turlock, California. Brenda Barrows (sister-in-law of Cliff Barrows of the Billy Graham Evangelistic Association) had been struggling to receive the baptism of the Holy Spirit. I did not know she was there, but the Holy Spirit was planning to give her a sign that would release her from fear and free her to receive this blessing.

I walked into the prayer room hours before the service was to begin. In my mind I saw a young woman, who wanted to be baptized in the Holy Spirit, surrounded by six people who were giving her instructions on how to receive the baptism. I arranged seven chairs in the room in a circle around a little pulpit. I would be standing there explaining to them that I knew this meeting was going to take place and that the woman would receive the Holy Spirit baptism. Then I saw five people who would interrupt us as we were praying. For these five curious people who would come in one at a time, I placed five chairs against the wall.

I forgot about this incident until the end of the service that evening. I asked for persons in the service who wanted to be baptized in the Holy Spirit to come forward. Several people came to the altar to receive the baptism; among them was the girl I had seen in my mind. She prayed and talked, but nothing seemed to happen.

After about an hour, Brenda Barrows started to leave. Several girls had been praying with her. I asked them to go to the prayer room and wait for me there. Then I approached Brenda. "If God gave you a sign that He was really going to fill you with His Spirit, that it was His will to do so, and that you can receive the baptism of the Holy Spirit, would you give Him that chance? Would you be willing to give me the opportunity to at least show you that He's interested in you? That he wants to release you from these problems and doubts you have regarding Him?"

Reluctantly she gave in. We went back to the prayer room where six people were waiting for us. She was number seven.

I asked them to sit in the seven chairs that had already been placed around the pulpit. "I've arranged these seven chairs because I knew you were going to be here tonight. I knew about the problem you are having concerning the baptism in the Holy Spirit. And these six people are here to talk about it. When they have finished, their thoughts will fit together like a puzzle into a description of who the Holy

Spirit really is and how He will baptize you."

The six women offered their observations. Then we stood together and began praying. I laid hands on the young woman and felt real victory. Someone walked into the room. I told the seven not to be startled, that there would be four more who would come and sit in the five chairs I had arranged against the wall. As others wandered in, I would stop and explain to them all exactly what was happening, what we were doing together.

We prayed for some time but the fifth person did not arrive. As we were praying, everyone gave advice as to how to receive the baptism and what it should really mean to a Christian. But nothing happened. I was beginning to feel defeated. *This is going to look bad*, I thought. So I left the prayer room and went home exhausted.

The next day, my wife Gloria and I were eating with friends at a restaurant. At another table were some people from the church. Among them was one of the six girls who had prayed with us in the prayer room the previous evening.

"How are you doing?" I asked.

"Fine," she answered. "Did you hear what happened last night?"

"Well, no. What happened?"

"Brenda was filled with the Holy Spirit."

"She was? That's great!"

"Yes, we just had to wait for the fifth person, that's all. Right after you left, the fifth person came in."

In Albany, Oregon, I was involved in a seminar at Evangel Church where the Rev. Hubert Book is pastor. Prior to the service the Holy Spirit began to speak to me about a young man who would be in the audience. He was quite depressed with his job situation and wanted a change. He had been praying for some time but he was confused and did not know what to do. I could see the young man in my imagination—he was wearing a yellow shirt. I made a note of the details and walked out into the sanctuary.

As I was sitting on the platform, a Scripture kept coming to my mind: Psalms 37:4 "Delight thyself also in the Lord; And He shall give thee the desires of thine heart" (KJV).

Lord, I prayed, *does this mean that you are going to give him a new job or that he should make a change?*

There seemed to be no answer. *I am presuming a lot,* I thought to myself. *I don't even know if there is a man in a yellow shirt here; and if there is one, I don't know if he is dissatisfied with his career.*

At the conclusion of the service, I was immediately confronted by a young married couple. The man was wearing a short-sleeved yellow shirt.

"There's something special I've been praying about," he began.

"I know," I said, interrupting him. Then I explained what had happened. "Let me give you a Scripture," I said. "Delight thyself also in the Lord and He shall give you the desires of your heart."

Later, on the way home, the pastor talked with me about the words I had written prior to the service regarding this young member of his congregation. After discussing the gifts of the Holy Spirit for a few minutes, he asked me about the Scripture I had given the man, Psalms 37:4.

"Was that a prophecy?" he asked. "I mean, are you suggesting that God will give him a new career?"

"I don't know," I answered frankly.

Two months later, Gloria and I received a letter from the Rev. Hubert Book in which he wrote, "Remember the man you prayed with? The one with the yellow shirt? Well, he has a new job!"

The story of Edward Hagle, a forty-year-old science teacher in Florence, Oregon, is a dramatic one. He stands six feet, two inches tall. With shoulder length hair and wide-eyed curiosity, he resembles an Italian movie director's idea of a mad scientist.

Hagle is something of a genius. He sold his commercial fishing business in November 1969, and put his talents to work as an inventor. In a short time, he was turning out dozens of inventions from kitchen equipment to family games. He and his sponsors were turning a very nice profit.

But Hagle's heart was in a more humanitarian project. He wanted to develop a portable device that would enable the deaf, dumb and blind to communicate. After months of hard work, his dream began to take on a practical look. But his sponsors were not willing to invest thousands of dollars in an idea that promised no quick return. Hagle was on his own again. He joined the staff of a local High School in Florence, Oregon, but his salary could hardly finance the enormous project on his hands. Hagle also envisioned a large community for the deaf and blind. This idea struck a chord of interest with the clergy in his own Catholic church.

In the winter of 1971, the Hagles came in

contact with Jesuit priests who were abandoning a monastery near Peekskill, New York. Hagle was becoming convinced that God was with him, that his invention would succeed. But just as the project neared completion, he encountered additional expenses. He fell short by five hundred dollars. Mr. Hagle couldn't bear to see his invention floundering for the lack of such a small sum of money. There was nothing to do but wait.

Hagle didn't have to wait long. On Friday night, March 24, 1972, a miracle happened. It involved the gift of prophecy.

Earlier in the week Henry Johnson, a Pentecostal layman, had invited Hagle to a special charismatic seminar in the city. Hagle had had no intention of going, but on this particular night he felt strangely compelled to attend church.

Before the seminar I was seated at a desk in Pastor David Womersley's study. He left me to lead the congregational singing. I was alone for a few minutes. Then came the overwhelming feeling of warmth and love of Christ's presence filling that little study.

The Holy Spirit began to speak. *There is a man who will visit the church tonight. He will be dressed in blue. He will sit on your left at the back of the auditorium. Prophesy to him. Tell him that I will solve his financial problem! Tell him that I am God.*

I wrote the message down on paper, took a Bible from the pastor's bookshelf, slipped the paper inside, and left the Bible laying there on the desk.

When I walked out onto the platform I was disappointed. There were a lot of men present in the filled church, but no one was wearing a blue suit except the pastor. I laughed a little at myself for being such a mystic.

Fifteen minutes later, Ed Hagle walked in. Later I learned that he was late because at the last minute he had decided to change his clothes. He took a seat at the back of the auditorium on my left. He was wearing a blue suit.

At the conclusion of the service I called to him. "There is someone here tonight with a unique financial problem. I have a message for you from God." Hagle responded and walked to the front of the auditorium. I was amazed at his composure. He came to the platform and spoke into the microphone. He told us part of his story. He told us that he needed God's help to finish his work. It was hard to believe that he was a Roman Catholic visiting a Protestant church for the first time.

But Hagle soon lost his "cool." I told him

how I had seen him in my mind before the service; how I had known of his special need. I sent h: .1 with Pastor Womersley back into the study to bring out the large Bible that I had placed on the desk. They returned to the platform with the Bible. "Turn to Matthew, chapter seven, and read verse seven." Edward flipped through the pages, found my note and read it aloud to the congregation. He was quite excited when he finally found the right verse: "Ask, and it shall be given to you."

Then I prophesied to him. I told him how God would prove Himself to him, and that God must be very interested in his project because He was going to help him.

"If you should suddenly receive the money you need, will you give God the benefit of a doubt and say that He was responsible?" I asked.

Hagle nodded his head in affirmation. And then to make doubly sure, I asked him to look at me. "Are you sure? Will you give God the glory when He sends the money?" I asked.

"Oh, yes!" Hagle answered enthusiastically.

I invited the audience to participate in a miracle. "Let's praise the Lord as though God had already answered this prayer," I said.

As a matter of fact, He had! Jerry

Knudsen, a local banker who was in the church that night, recently had cashed in an investment at a substantial profit. After fulfilling his obligations to the church, he felt like giving God a special offering of five hundred dollars.

Yet he had some doubts about what was happening that night. It had all been a little too fast for him. After thoroughly checking out my credentials—and Hagle's—Knudsen believed that God was indeed at work.

Three days later, Hagle received a check for five hundred dollars. His dream was still alive.

In March 1974 two years later, I received a long distance phone call from the Rev. Cliff Emery, the new pastor of that church. "Do you remember a Catholic visitor who attended the conference you held here in 1972?" he asked.

"Ed Hagle," I answered.

"Yes. You must also remember the story involved. Well, last week he finally received his patent. They may manufacture the product right here in this city."

I returned to Florence the following Monday and spoke to a special audience of curious citizens. Once again we thanked God for the miracle He had begun two years before. We also prayed a special prayer for Ed Hagle who dedicated his life to Christ. That night he experienced a new language of praise.

There have been many occasions when the voice of the Spirit has told me what was going to happen in a conference workshop. For example, one night during a workshop which I conducted in Boca Raton, Florida, the Holy Spirit began to show me what was going to happen at the conclusion of the service. A number of people were going to come to the front of the church to ask for prayer. Some of them had special spiritual needs, others were praying about their health or their children. The picture was so clear that I could actually count the people. There were fifteen. In my imagination I invited the pastor to join with us. The fifteen people, the pastor and I prayed together.

The Holy Spirit spoke to me: *Prophesy to these people and bless them. Tell them that I love them. Tell them that I have chosen them to be your partners in prayer for this conference. Now look around you and count the people.*

I glanced around. There were seventeen of us.

The Holy Spirit continued to speak within me, *Write on paper the things that you have seen. It will happen.*

By faith I believed that it was the Spirit

of God who had spoken to me. I wrote, "Ask the pastor to join you. Pray together. There will be seventeen of you." I also wrote part of the prophecy the Lord had given me.

It was an especially joyous service that night. Though our gathering was not large, Christians of all denominations were involved.

The conclusion of the service happened just as the Lord had shown me. I watched helplessly as the people in the congregation were deciding whether they wanted to come to the front for special prayer or remain in their seats. I shared with no one the vision or impression God had given me of the altar service. Fifteen people responded.

I invited the Rev. Dean Gross, pastor, to join us. The seventeen of us prayed, then I shared with them the things that God had shown me prior to the service.

However, I don't believe this part of the service was more important than any other. Worship was not centered around this or any other gift; it was directed entirely toward Jesus Christ. The structure of our worship was not dependent upon such a gift, but it did allow for it. All of us left feeling that God had gently spoken to us through the experience.

Looking back on such moments in my ministry, I am pleased that people have been encouraged or helped. Yet, I have difficulty myself in classifying the gift at work. I can understand why many Catholic charismatic leaders consider this a prophetic gift.

13

The Spirit and Guidance

Listening to the voice of the Holy Spirit for personal guidance is wrought with many hazards.

I already have mentioned the fine line between the popular definition of the gift of the word of knowledge and the gift of prophecy. If someone should predict that you will someday be a missionary to Ghana they are prophesying. Of course the prophecy would have to fulfill the four requirements I previously have outlined. However, if someone should tell you that God has informed him that you should go to Ghana as a missionary, he is claiming to have a word of knowledge for you from the Lord. He is attempting to force you into a personal decision on the basis of his revelation. If it is truly of God, He will reveal His will to you also.

Mr. and Mrs. Leonard Johnson of Boca Raton, Florida, experienced this kind of divine guidance. Johnson lost his job as a general contractor and for several months had sought work. Occasionally the Johnsons attended a living room prayer group in the Miami area. The leader of the group was a mysterious charismatic lady who told Leonard that the Lord had given her a word of knowledge. *Call Mr. Robert Ferguson. Ask him for a job.*

Johnson knew that Ferguson was an executive in a large Florida corporation, and was active in the charismatic movement in Florida. But Johnson had only heard of Ferguson; they had never met.

The Johnsons were Methodists, and they were new to the charismatic movement. Yet they did not naively believe everything they were told. After several days of personal debate, Johnson concluded that there could be no possible harm in contacting Robert Ferguson, so he telephoned.

At this point the story begins to sound far-fetched. But it is a true example of how complex the outworking of God's will often is. Weeks before, Ferguson had attended a large conference on the charismatic movement in Bradenton, Florida. One afternoon while walking across the conference grounds, Ferguson saw a torn and weather-stained business card lying on the grass. Almost subconsciously he picked it up and glanced at it. It read: Leonard Johnson, General Contractor, Boca Raton, Florida. Ferguson slipped the card into his billfold.

Several weeks later, Ferguson received a telephone call from Leonard Johnson who said he was a Spirit-filled, out-of-work Methodist businessman. The name Leonard Johnson buzzed around in Ferguson's mind for a moment.

"No, I'm sorry," he said. "We do employ several contractors but to my knowledge the jobs are all filled."

Days later, Ferguson and other corporation executives were invited to a special business meeting. Among the decisions which had to be made that day was the hiring of new personnel.

"Anybody know a good general contractor?"

Ferguson was momentarily stunned. *Perhaps the Lord is opening up a job for the Methodist man who telephoned me,* he thought. On the other hand he didn't know the man and to recommend him was rather risky. *What was his name?* Ferguson asked himself. Suddenly he remembered the name on the business card—Leonard Johnson. *It must be the Lord.*

"I know one!" he said loudly. He pulled the tattered business card from his billfold. Johnson eventually was hired.

Throughout this complex series of events, Johnson never once told Ferguson about the Miami woman who had given him a word of knowledge and had advised him to contact Robert Ferguson.

It seems that, as a rule, God does not give guidance to another individual concerning your life. Jesus once told Peter what would happen to him when he became an older man.

"What about John," Peter asked. "What will happen to him?"

"What is that to you?" Jesus replied.

On the other hand, many times the Holy Spirit will use someone else to confirm His revelation to you. The Apostle Paul at one time had persecuted the Christians. Jesus appeared to him as a great light on the road to Damascus (Acts 9). Paul, struck down and blinded, was told to go into Damascus and wait. For three days he waited without eating or drinking.

As Paul was praying, God showed him a Christian named Ananias. Paul had never seen him before, but in his vision Ananias came to him and laid hands on him to heal him. Paul did not ask his aides to find Ananias and bring him in. Instead, the Holy Spirit spoke to Ananias and told him Paul's story.

When these two men met, their personal revelations were an overwhelming confirmation to each other. Paul's story was identical to what the Holy Spirit had already shown Ananias. Both men must have been awed by the omniscience of God.

During a seminar in Albany, Oregon, I called out to the audience, "There is a young man in the balcony. You have been putting off a decision. You already know God's will. You asked him for a sign and He gave it to you. What are you afraid of? Go ahead. God will use you in whatever you pursue."

Two days later I was approached by Steve Covey. "The other night you pointed right at me," he said. "I have known God's will for some time and have been putting it off. That gave me the added confidence to go ahead."

How should you respond to a personal

prophecy or to someone who claims to give you a word of knowledge in the name of the Lord? I believe that Mary gives us the best example. When shepherds found her in Bethlehem, they told how the sky was filled with angels describing the birth of a Savior. The wise men came from many miles to give gifts. The stars which had been charted for centuries proclaimed the birth.

How did Mary respond to these dramatic events? She did not use them in brag sessions with other mothers. She did not become anxious when Jesus was twenty-nine years old and only a carpenter's apprentice. Mary kept in her heart these revelations of others, even her own miraculous experiences.

I believe that Mary's response is the right one. If someone tells you to go to Ghana to be a missionary, don't pack your bags. Keep it in your heart. If God speaks to you and confirms the revelation from other sources, it will happen. Remember that you will be held responsible for your own decisions.

My conclusion is that Christians should be open to revelation. It can be a part of the decision-making process, but it should never be the only source of guidance.

Jim Cravens was leading a prayer service at Melodyland Christian Center in Anaheim, California, when the Holy Spirit began to speak to him about someone in the audience.

Cravens waited until the service had concluded, then approached a middle-aged woman. "The Lord wanted me to tell you to get out of the business you are in!" he announced.

The woman was horrified by Cravens's boldness. How could he know what God's will was for her? True, she was in a competitive business which she had considered leaving. But the young man's boldness shocked her. She didn't like the idea of him speaking to her about God's will.

"You're wondering how to know whether my words are really of God or not?" continued Cravens. "Let me tell you something. These are your sisters you are sitting with. You are not the oldest but they look to you as a leader."

The woman's mouth dropped open in astonishment.

Cravens turned to one of the other sisters. "If you keep up this relationship which has begun with this man in your life, you will lose your husband and divide your family. Get away from him!"

That was the clincher! They all knew of

their sister's infatuation with another man.

The woman did get out of the business and later looked up Cravens to tell an amazing story of how God had saved her from financial disaster. Her business was involved in a pyramid sales scheme. Only weeks after she sold out the market became so saturated that sales actually came to a standstill. She would have lost everything.

Sometimes the voice of the Spirit comes as a sign to give direction.

When I was working on the manuscript for the book, *Tonight They'll Kill a Catholic*, I realized that I would have to return to Northern Ireland to collect more information. I knew the trip would be dangerous since I would be contacting several militant groups. Gloria couldn't go this time and I didn't want to go alone. I asked God to give me a partner for the adventure.

Gloria and I began a seminar in Waukegan, Illinois, only days before I had to confirm my flight reservations to Belfast. The pastor who was co-ordinating the seminar had a son, Roger Heuser, who was the Christian education director of the church.

During the week, I joked with Pastor Heuser and his family about the possibility of Roger joining me in Northern Ireland. None of us thought it would happen. For one thing, it would be an impossibility from a financial standpoint. I was in the process of raising my own support for the trip.

Later in the week I considered it more seriously. Gloria thought that it was a good idea. She did not want me to go alone. I prayed and God said, "He is the one."

Yet I wondered, *How will God arrange everything in such a short time?*

One night prior to the seminar, I was praying in one of the church offices. The Holy Spirit began to prepare me for something very special which He had planned for that evening. He said, *Roger is going to go with you to Northern Ireland and tonight I will show you that it is My will!*

That evening I planned to ask people to pledge to pray for me each day that I was away. *When you call for prayer partners, there will be twenty-eight who will stand with you,* the voice of the Spirit said. I wrote it down on paper, of course, and put the note on the desk.

That evening, everything unfolded exactly as the Holy Spirit had shown me. Without telling anyone what I felt God had told me or without any prompting, twenty-eight persons pledged to pray daily for me. I invited them to the front and we joined hands to form a circle. Then I told them how the Holy Spirit had been speaking to me about the trip. I told them that Roger was going to go too. I sent Roger with another friend back to the church office to retrieve my note. He read it to the audience. Then I invited the twenty-eight people to surround him and we prayed that God would use him on the trip. Looking back to that moment, I suppose it all seemed a bit absurd. Roger still had no money to make the trip.

"Of course, this will cost some money," I told the audience. Before I realized it, I was committing myself. "I'll give $100. If there are nine more who will do this, his trip will be paid for."

The nine stood immediately. One of them was Gillie Stoddart, leader of a local charismatic prayer group. She had heard of the seminar earlier in the day and had decided to cancel her own prayer group to join ours. Mrs. Stoddart had received some rather strange instructions which she believed to be from the Lord. She had felt prompted to stop by the bank and withdraw $100. When I presented the special project she responded immediately, confident that it was God's will.

Another young man had been debating

for some time the Scriptural teaching on tithing. After several years of hearing theologians and teachers discuss the subject, he had finally made up his own mind. That very week he had decided to begin to support his church financially. He had always admired the work of associate pastor Roger Heuser, who he believed was underpaid, so he decided to begin by giving $100 to him. The check already had been filled out when I called for the nine people to support Roger's trip to Ireland.

Similar stories came from the others. No one doubted that God's sovereign will was involved.

Finally, the voice of the Spirit may come in the form of a warning to give direction and guidance.

When Syria was at war against Israel in Old Testament times, God prepared His people for battle. Each time the Syrians planned an ambush for the Israeli troops, God sent a message to the Jews, and warned them of the impending attacks. Naturally, the Syrian king was distraught by the possibility that his tactical secrets were being divulged by some traitor. But there was no traitor; God's messenger Elisha the prophet was faithfully delivering the warnings from God to the king of Israel. When the Syrian king heard of Elisha he was so convinced of the power of the prophet that he did everything possible to capture him. But God delivered Elisha from the enemy.

While I have stressed the importance of common sense when trying to determine the will of God, I also suggest that we should remain sensitive to God's voice. An angel appeared to Joseph and warned him to flee Israel. Joseph took his family and fled to Egypt. Thus the baby Jesus survived King Herod's attempt to murder him.

Do not rule out the possibility that God's voice may speak to you in an emergency.

After all, God loves us.

Bibliography

Brumback, Carl. *Suddenly from Heaven.* Springfield, MO: Gospel Publishing House, 1961.

Frost, Robert. *Aglow with the Spirit.* Northridge, CA: Voice Publications.

Garrett, Eileen J., editor. *Beyond the Five Senses.* (especially the chapter "Faith Healing at Lourdes" and "Diagnosis: Miracle") Philadelphia, New York: J. B. Lippincott Co., 1957.

Gee, Donald. *Concerning Spiritual Gifts.* Springfield, MO: Gospel Publishing House, 1937.

Harper, Michael. *Power for the Body of Christ.* Watchung, NJ: Watchung Book Sales.

Kendrick, Klaude. *The Promise Fulfilled: A History of the Modern Pentecostal Movement.* Springfield, MO: Gospel Publishing House, 1961.

Kuhlman, Kathryn. *God Can Do It Again.* Englewood Cliffs, NJ: Prentice-Hall, 1969.
--*I Believe in Miracles.* Englewood Cliffs, NJ: Prentice-Hall, 1962.

Leuret, Frankcois and Henri Bon. *Modern Miraculous Cures.* New York: Farrar, Straus & Cudahy, 1957.

Neal, Emily Gardiner. *A Reporter Finds God through Spiritual Healing.* New York: Morehouse-Barlow Co., 1956.

O'Connor, Edward, C.S.C. *The Pentecostal Movement in the Catholic Church.* Notre Dame: Ava Maria Press, 1971. (A thorough account of the history and theology of Catholic Pentecostalism in America. A "must" reference book for every pastor's library.)

Rhine, Louisa E. *ESP in Life and Lab.* New York: Macmillan Co., 1967.

Roberts, Oral. *If You Need Healing Do These Things.* Tulsa: Healing Waters, 1954.

Sherrill, John. *They Speak with Other Tongues.* New York: Pyramid Books, 1965.

Stern, Karl. *The Third Revolution.* New York: Harcourt, Brace and Co., 1954.

Tournier, Paul. *The Healing of Persons.* New York: Harper and Row, 1965.

Van Dusen, H. P. "The Third Force in Christendom," *Life* (June 9, 1958), pp. 113-124.

Weathershead, Leslie D. *Psychology in the Service of the Soul.* London: Epworth Press, 1929.
  --*Psychology, Religion and Healing.* New York, Nashville: Abingdon Press, 1951.

Woodard, Christopher. *A Doctor Heals by Faith.* London: Max Parrish and Co., 1965.